Initiation Song from the Finders' Lodge

Please bring strange things.
Please come bringing new things.
Let very old things come into your hands.
Let what you do not know come into your eyes.
Let desert sand harden your feet.
Let the arch of your feet be the mountains.
Let the paths of your fingertips be your maps
and the ways you go be the lines on your palms.
Let there be deep snow in your inbreathing
and your outbreath be the shining of ice.
May your mouth contain the shapes of strange words.
May you smell food cooking you have not eaten.
May the spring of a foreign river be your navel.
May your soul be at home where there are no houses.
Walk carefully, well loved one,
walk mindfully, well loved one,
walk fearlessly, well loved one.
Return with us, return to us,
be always coming home.

– Ursula K. Le Guin

Always Coming Home (1985)

LIVING THE SIGNS

PISCES

THE DREAMER

PR 12.22

ISBN: 979-8-9861770-2-1

Written by Britten LaRue
@brittenlarue

Publication Design & Illustrations
by Angela George
@bygeorgepartners

Published by In Case of Emergence
www.incaseofemergence.com
@incaseof.emergence

Living the Signs: Pisces is intended as a
guide and source of inspiration to help
anyone looking for alternative, intuitive,
and more nature-based frameworks
for living in rhythmic time, practicing
self-care at home, and learning more
about the language of astrology and the
tarot. It is not intended as a substitute
for professional therapy or professional
medical attention.

The information provided here is not
meant to serve as the only source of
information on these topics. Readers
are encouraged not to make any life
decisions based solely on the
information herein.

This journal is entirely self-published by
the author, Britten LaRue, and her design
collaborator, Angela George. Please for-
give typographical errors and technical
inaccuracies as the result of well-meaning
human beings.

Living the Signs: Astrology for Radiant Embodiment
is a series of twelve workbooks
co-created by astrologer Britten LaRue
and designer Angela George.

Across the scope of each, we aim to inspire your mind,
nourish your heart, and enchant your spirit with ancient
symbols for the modern world.

Living the Signs supports the reader to gently de-program from
unhelpful conditioning, grow trust in change,
come home to the wild soul, and embrace radical self-love.

Cheers!
Britten + Angela

We dedicate this workbook to all Pisces Suns,
especially my Grampa, Carl Ahlgren, the most skillfully Jupiterian person I've ever known,
(Britten), and to my first two loves, my father Hugo MonDragon and my brother Shon, two
Pisces dreamers that have always inspired and encouraged me to dream big (Angela).

USING THE WORKBOOK

**THE CONTENTS OF THIS BOOK ARE DIVIDED
INTO THREE PARTS** ·······································

Ways we approach the sign, with interactive
opportunities for self-inquiry throughout

Creative and spiritual rituals and activities

Journaling space at the back for your doodles,
tarot spreads, notes, diagrams, and lists

The topics here are not linear, and thus you are
encouraged to hop around and leap between
the sections.

Go ahead and peek at those suggested rituals and
activities now so that you can start doing what
inspires you from the beginning.

Trust that you will find your way to the order that
makes the most sense for you.

Have fun! This is your book. There is no right
or wrong way to use it.

Make it pleasurable.

Make it nourishing.

Make it support the unfolding
of your authentic self.

TABLE OF CONTENTS

LIVING THE SIGNS

Astrology for Radiant Embodiment

Astrology is a technology of attunement. It is a tool to help us talk to ourselves more lovingly, compassionately, and thus effectively. The language of astrology encourages us to awaken and remember what is wondrous, glorious, funny, poignant, and heroic about our human experience. When we Live the Signs, as I like to say, we shake life into all the facets of who we are here to be. We come home to who we are on a spirit level.

WHEN YOU CEDE YOUR SIGNS TO OTHERS, YOU BLOCK YOUR FLOW. AND WHEN YOUR FLOW IS OBSTRUCTED IN THAT SIGN ENERGY, YOU MIGHT EXPRESS ITS UNSKILLFUL "SHADOW" NATURE.

Our birth chart is a snapshot of the moment we were born. In that moment, the Sun was only in one of the 12 signs. The Sun is an important part of who you are, but you are also the whole of the sky! The other planets were scattered around the other signs, and you are anchored into those sign energies as well. The 12 "houses" (pie pieces) of a birth chart represent spheres of life, like departments of human experience. And each of your houses is governed by one of the 12 signs.

Thus — you are all 12 signs!

If we can agree that the whole of the 12 signs speaks to the entirety of human personality — our various needs, capacities, desires, and goals — then in order to round out all of the possibilities of who we can be, we must lean into all of the signs.

The foundation of my framework for *Living the Signs* has to do with waking up the part of self that is each sign in order to know ourselves more fully, more radiantly, and more creatively.

It is my observation, from both my personal experience as a human and as an intuitive guide for others, that one of the primary reasons for disenchantment in life is that we fall into only a handful of roles and guises, and we allow other people to play our signs for us.

When you cede your signs to others, you block your flow. And when your flow is obstructed in that sign energy, you might express its unskillful "shadow" nature.

The primary objective for *Living the Signs* is to share what I've learned about embodying each sign energy to support you in aligning with all the signs of your emotional, mental, physical, and spiritual body. See your journey with each sign on a spectrum that is neither good nor bad, but rather more skillful to less skillful. Thus, what we're going for here is to feel more skillful at being each sign.

You can use this workbook absolutely any time of year, though it is extra supportive to work with each sign during its Sun season. Take your time with it. Be gentle to it. Be patient with it. Think of this workbook as part of you ... because it is! There is no rush to more skillfully awaken the part of you that is each sign. The dosage will always be what it needs to be.

Enjoy!

*QUOTES

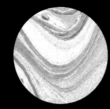

Mystery is at the heart of creativity. That, and surprise... As creative channels, we need to trust the darkness.

— Julia Cameron, Pisces Sun

"

I'm free. I just do what I want, say what I want, say how I feel, and I don't try to hurt nobody. I just try to make sure that I don't compromise my art in any kind of way, and I think people respect that.

— Erykah Badu, Pisces Sun and Moon

Please go for your dreams. Whatever your ideals, you can become whatever you want to become.

— Michael Jackson, Pisces Rising & Moon

I've always sung in the shower. Now I make the stage a mental shower in order not to get too uptight and enjoy it.

— Elizabeth Taylor, Pisces Sun, Mercury, Mars, & North Node

You've got a song you're singing from your gut, you want that audience to feel it in their gut. And you've got to make them think that you're one of them sitting out there with them too. They've got to be able to relate to what you're doing.

— Johnny Cash, Pisces Sun, Rising, Mercury, Mars, & North Node

I am an excitable person who only understands life lyrically, musically, in whom feelings are much stronger as reason. I am so thirsty for the marvelous that only the marvelous has power over me. Anything I cannot transform into something marvelous, I let go. Reality doesn't impress me. I only believe in intoxication, in ecstasy, and when ordinary life shackles me, I escape, one way or another. No more walls.

— Anaïs Nin, Pisces Sun and Venus

You have to work hard for it, but first you have to want it, and then you have to dream on it.

— Liza Minelli, Pisces Sun

Punk is musical freedom. It's saying, doing and playing what you want. In Webster's terms, 'nirvana' means freedom from pain, suffering and the external world, and that's pretty close to my definition of Punk Rock.

— Kurt Cobain, Pisces Sun, Mercury, Venus, & Saturn

Dragonfly out in the sun you know what I mean, don't you know
Butterflies all havin' fun you know what I mean
Sleep in peace when day is done
That's what I mean

And this old world is a new world
And a bold world
For me

Stars when you shine you know how I feel
Scent of the pine you know how I feel
Oh freedom is mine
And I know how I feel

— Nina Simone, Pisces Sun, Mercury, & North Node

ATTUNING TO PISCES:

WAYS WE APPROACH THE SIGN

BEFORE DIVING IN ...

Give yourself a clear one-sentence intention for your commitment to this workbook. What would you like to learn, and how would you like to grow from exploring the energy of Pisces? What is Pisces to you now, here at the beginning? Free-write whatever comes to mind when you think of Pisces.

*
Extra space for all journaling prompts can be found at the back of the workbook.

Signs are energies. They describe the nature of the energies with which you do or are anything: how to inhabit your body, create, make love, present an argument, organize, study, nurture, and heal. They are adverbs for characterizing the essence of how you do you in various fields of life.

It is impossible to trap a sign, especially not this one, with a single phrasing. Rather we track it, we reach for it, and feel its slick, slithery skin between our hands before it slips away again. It is in the process that we find pleasure.

This is how symbolic language works. Free from the shackles of denotation, symbol is open and multivalent, in that it carries always more than one meaning at once. The human psyche has yearned for symbol and myth since the beginning.

Symbols are animated thought-images that resonate on many levels of understanding at once. Astrology, depth psychology, dream tending, shamanic journeying, and story-telling all activate our desire for symbol. It is both crucial and more pleasurable to allow a single term like "Pisces" to be infinitely holographic.

Here in these pages we will aim to catch the uncatchable by approaching it in various ways, each one with nuances that will stimulate your imagination and bring you a little closer to appreciating the part of you that is:

THE IDEALIST

THE MAGICAL CHILD

THE SHAPESHIFTER

THE MYSTIC

THE NUMINOUS ONE

If Pisces is about anything, it's about the gifts of attunement. What does this word suggest to you? What does it mean to be "attuned to" someone, something, or the environment?

How do you "tune in" to yourself, to your imagination and your dreams, to other people, to the energy of the spaces you inhabit?

To commit to Pisces for an extended period of time, turn to the suggested activities and rituals later in this book. Build an altar to Pisces. Begin to track your dreams. Experiment with the New Moon ritual with Pisces (especially potent in Pisces season but

available to your imagination at any time of year). Play with the Pledge to Pisces exercise on a daily basis for however long it feels good for you.

Before diving in any further, you will likely want to cast your birth chart, if you've never done so before. You will want as close as possible to an EXACT birth time and city. Once you know these, go to *chart.chaninicholas.com*. There you can input your birth time, see your chart, and learn some rudimentary things about it.

For the purposes of this workbook, you will especially want to locate the following:

- *What house you have the sign of Pisces: this is where you are most Piscean*

- *What planets or points you have in Pisces, if any: these will determine how you do Pisces*

- *What sign and house you have Neptune, infusing Piscean energy into that house as well*

- *What sign and planets do you have in the 12th House: these relate to Pisces themes*

PISCES IN YOUR CHART

In which house do you have Pisces?
Which department of life is that? SEE APPENDIX.

Do you feel yourself to be more sensitive, empathic,
and imaginative in that part of your life?

Which planets or points show up in your chart in
the sign of Pisces?

What does that planet or point signify? SEE APPENDIX.

In which sign and house do you have your natal Jupiter?
Which department of life is that? SEE APPENDIX.

Does it resonate for you that this is the department
of life where you are most likely to feel fortunate,
experience abundance and "a lot"-ness, and/or over-
stretch yourself to do more?

In which sign and house do you have your natal
Neptune? Which department of life is that? SEE APPENDIX.

Does it resonate for you that this is the department of
life where you are most likely to feel into fantasy,
spirituality, naiveté, and idealism?

Does Neptune sit next to any other planets? If so, which?
What do those planets, if any, signify? SEE APPENDIX.

Having Neptune next to those planets will give a more
creative, compassionate, and intuitive quality to how you
express them.

When astrologers read your chart, part of what they are doing is feeling into what it would be like to have a given sign in a certain house with particular planets and/or points. You can try to think it through analytically, but it's better left to your intuition.

As you feel into how all of this information describes you, it should be like: "Ah yes, I know this in myself" not "Oh, I guess this is how I am." The chart isn't telling you who you are. You know who you are. The chart helps to reflect and contextualize things you already feel are true, and gifts you another language for considering them.

You can explore your chart more as you go deeper into this workbook and the other workbooks of this series. For now, just let what you're learning "sit in your back pocket" and "simmer on the side burner," as I like to say. I used to always want to know everything immediately and right away, and it's been a really great practice for my analytical mind to trust that concepts and ideas can just simmer, percolate, and bubble up as they will.

INVENTORY OF THE PRESENT MOMENT: ATTUNING TO PISCES

I like the phrasing "inventory of the present moment." It suggests that you are noticing, taking stock, and listing what is available for you right now, right here, in the present moment. You are not being asked to analyze or judge or explain. This list is only attached to present circumstances, and is allowed to shift and evolve over time. Remember: you are allowed to change.

What does this word 'attunement ' suggest to you?

What does it mean to be "attuned to" someone, something, or the environment?

How do you "tune in" to yourself, to your imagination and your dreams, to other people, to the energy of the spaces you inhabit?

CORRESPONDENCES FOR PISCES AND NEPTUNE

AN ALTAR FOR PISCES

Whether we call it a "sacred space," or "altar," or "special spot," the idea is to gather together objects that remind you of the energy-thought-form to which you want to connect.

The idea is to gather together objects that remind you of Pisces. Be open to the fact that you may not know at the beginning exactly how this will feel for you, how it'll look, how you will use it, or how you will enjoy it.

With your altar, you are drawing happy, focused energy toward one place. The more you sit there with your journal or to meditate or to draw/create or to just relax and daydream, the more that spot will be charged with good feelings.

INVITING IN CORRESPONDENCES

The idea behind correspondences is that symbolic forms such as signs / planets attune with other forms of available energies, and that corresponding energy forms are more powerful when resonating together. Types of things to consider for correspondences: colors, herbs, spices, crystals, gods/goddesses, elements, seasons, months, signs, tarot cards, planets, oils, foods, art forms, animals, birds, insects, runes, days of week, chakras, myths, and stories.

It is helpful, healing, and good practice to seek out correspondences that most relate to the lands, culture, and belief systems of your blood lineage. Embrace and enjoy the process of your own resourcefulness.

SEA-BASED ITEMS: Shells, coral, pearls, driftwood, a bowl of sand, and anything else that reminds you of water

COLORS: Blue, purple, and sea green

CRYSTALS: Labradorite, amethyst, fluorite, turquoise, sapphire, aquamarine, jade, moonstone

PLANTS & SEAWEED: Water lily, plants that grow near water, kelp such as bladderwrack, moss, ferns, iris, evening primrose, opium poppy

CHAKRA: Crown

GODS & GODDESSES: Venus, Aphrodite, Diana, Neptune, Poseidon, Aegir, Vishnu, Jesus Christ, Dionysus

BIRDS: Stork, swan

WATER CREATURES: Seal, dolphin, fish, jellyfish

BODY PARTS: Feet, toes, veins, the psychic system

OTHER THINGS TO CONSIDER: Food, art, quotes on paper, photographs, magazine cutouts, books, fabrics, incense, ceramics honoring topics such as dreaming, the imagination, meditation, connecting to Spirit, music, poetry, watercolor, mermaids, lagoons, deltas, treasure at the bottom of the sea, fish, enlightenment, grace, forgiveness, mercy, love, compassion, illusion, altered states, meditation, clairvoyance, mysticism, and the dissolution of separateness

At the beginning, try to just get three items together to make a "family." Then aim to add something every few days as objects and ideas come to you (they will!) and soon your altar will be bursting with beauty and evocative energy.

Then start going there. You can start with just five minutes a day, perhaps while enjoying some dreamy music. And before you know it, you may find yourself called to this special spot more frequently and for longer spells.

My altar is a big tree stump about 5 inches high and 2 feet in diameter that I have on a small rug under the windows of my bedroom. I keep a few things that are "essential me" on there all of the time, and then I rotate out the other items based on what I'm working on in a given cycle.

Some believe that the altar serves as a "doorway" for Spirit to come through and likewise as a portal for us to speak to Spirit. As such, I sit there for all readings and recordings unless I'm out of town. Since I basically bring other people into my space when I do their recordings, I regularly clear the altar with the smoke of ethically harvested Palo Santo and sage so that it feels and smells refreshed.

I sincerely hope this is pleasurable (and even healing) for you!

SKILLFUL / NOT SKILLFUL:
ALIGNING WITH PISCES

The following are adjectives to describe Pisces, both skillfully and not skillfully. The purpose of identifying where we are skillful is to celebrate where we are in high frequency with the sign, so to speak. Yes, you are – in fact – already awesome.

The purpose of identifying where we are "not skillful" is not to feel bad about ourselves. No way. This is not about self-flagellation. What I've discovered is that wherever I'm feeling "not skillful," I recognize that it's not that I suck ("I knew it! Aha – proof!") or that I need to fix or banish some part of myself, it's that my access to the full breadth of the beauty of the sign energy got somehow stifled or blocked, or didn't think it had permission to play things any other way.

Honestly and compassionately, circle the adjectives that people might apply to you.

Then star those that you feel apply to you, whether or not anyone sees these in you in the outside world.

Note that Pisces is probably the least valued sign in our culture, so a lot of the adjectives here can easily fit into either category, or are only considered "unskillful" by people who don't appreciate these qualities. Adjust according to your intuition.

SKILLFUL:

Dreamy	Listening	Misunderstood	Loving	Intuitive
Empathic	Private	Shapeshifting	Forgiving	Idealistic
Imaginative	Mysterious	Emotional	Unknowable	Psychic
Yearning	Mystical	Spiritual	Musical	Poetic
Creative	Ancient	Open-hearted	Visionary	Humble
Healing	Childlike	Devoted	Romantic	Otherworldly

NOT SKILLFUL:

Escapist	Ungrounded	Secretive	Martyring	Co-dependent
Lying	Deceitful	Drifting	Melancholic	Addiction-prone
Delusional	Sacrificing	Procrastinating	Naïve	Identified with pain
Lost	Suffering	Victimized	Rose-colored glasses	
Flaky	Hypersensitive	Healer complex	Spiritual bypassing	

In what ways are you skillfully Piscean?

In what ways are you unskillfully playing Pisces?

Your energy follows your attention. If you give Pisces your attention, your energy will go to what you want. The more you direct your will to what you want, the more you will invite in the magical alchemy of growth, healing, and transformation. Naming what you want in a clear way is the most important first step.

FEEDING YOUR PISCES

When I was a mom with a toddler and a baby, I went to a "parent ed" talk to help me figure out how to get some scene control. There I learned a great concept: feeding the meter. The idea is that you give your irrational toddler your focused attention up front so that the child doesn't start demanding it, freaking out, and throwing a tantrum on the floor. Feed the meter all along, and your funny little human will be pleased and satisfied and less likely to escalate into a meltdown.

I've found this framework to be true with basically every part of my life, certainly with all of my close relationships.

I like to "feed my signs," so to speak, on a daily basis. During each sun sign season, I definitely give more of my attention to that particular sign, but I am always having conversations with the parts of me that are every sign.

The following is a list of ways you can feed your Pisces meter. Consider this an inventory for you to recognize the ways in which you are already showing up for your Pisces, as well as some ideas with which you can experiment in the future.

What else helps you connect with your Pisces?

Commit to at least one of these more regularly during the course of using this workbook. Whatever calls to you. Permission yourself to claim it as an important use of your time. And then enjoy!

When you aren't feeding your Pisces consciously, you will feed it unconsciously and thus unskillfully.

That can look like anything on this spectrum:

Too much Pisces can look like escapist and/or self-destructive behavior, secrecy/deception, lack of boundaries with other people, drifting through life without a clear path, playing the victim, inability to say no, trying to be all things to all people, addiction, martyring oneself, depression, invisibility, healer complex, lack of grounding

Too little Pisces can look like lack of compassion, low attunement to the feeling vibes of a space, rejection of childlike self, lack of imagination, dismissal of responsibility for nurturing or caretaking the world, denial of one's feeling body, dry pragmatism all day every day, disbelief in the power of idealism, inability to transcend the material plane through song, art, prayer, meditation, or play

It's definitely possible to be over-Pisces and under-Pisces at the same time. Be gentle with yourself as you consider where you are Pisces. I've struggled to be skillfully Pisces much of my life! What I've learned is that when you unskillfully express a sign energy, it's just because you weren't ever encouraged or didn't feel you had the right to be that sign in its fullness.

The goal of working with your unskillful nature is to ask it what it wants to be. For example: "escapism" wants to be "living with and in the dream." It's not about giving up dreams, in this case, but rather shifting the behavior so that it supports you more fully. With escapism, there's a fundamental lack of embodiment because the dream feels elsewhere. It is "not here," so we have to go somewhere else other than right here, in this body, in this moment, where we are now. And since we can only create a dream from the present moment where we're at, escapism blocks us from living the dream.

I have deep compassion for patterns of escapism because these used to rule my life. I couldn't break these until I began doing embodiment practices through energy healing, meditation, and somatic therapy.

ALL THE TIME   NEVER

Move the dial

- Meditation

- Journaling

- Zen practices like gardening or cooking
  or puzzles where you get into that flow
  space out of time

- Watching water flowing or a fire burning

- Standing in the shower and zoning out
  to the sound of the water

- Drawing- painting- singing- making art of any kind

- Tracking dreams in a dream diary

- Vision-boarding

- Stream-of-consciousness writing

- Poetry

- Deep prayer

- Dancing just to feel the music through you,
  not for exercise

- Gazing at the moon and the stars

- Long walks in solitude

- Love-making that merges two souls

- Falling asleep on the beach to the sound of the
  surf or under trees rustling in the wind or
  even against a window on a train...

SELF REFLECTION & INVENTORY

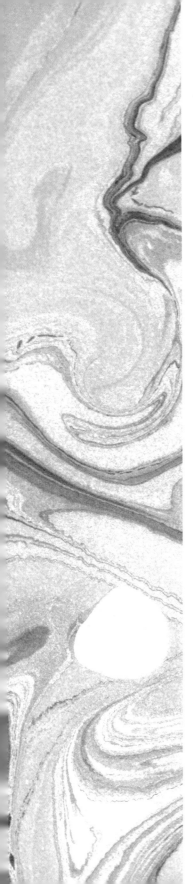

THE 12TH SIGN

Pisces is the last sign of the zodiac, thus it naturally carries within it the energy of endings, reflection and contemplating the past, letting go of attachments, and completing cycles.

The number 12 is a number that also resonates with endings. 12 hours in a day, 12 at night. 12 months in a year. 12 months to gestate, when we include the first 3 months post-partum that human babies need as part of that cycle.

After 12 we can go two ways: we can start over at 1, or we can slip into the mystery that is the number 13. Pisces – symbolized as two fish moving in opposite directions – is both the will back to 1 and the desire to know 13.

What part of you resonates with the idea of two fish swimming in opposite directions? The desire to reach toward the number 13 is the curiosity and yearning to know mystery, death, oneness with all life forms, to feel Spirit moving through us – this is like the fish swimming down to the delta, to be absorbed by the vast ocean.

It is a surrender of the ego.

The will back to number 1 is like the fish swimming upstream in order to spawn new life, regenerate, and start new cycles.

It is the ego trying to survive.

Let your contemplation begin with the knowing that Pisces IS the number 12 and all that that means to the imagination. Thus, it carries the mystery of 13 and the dream of 1.

What part of you dares to swim to the delta of the universal web of love?

What part of you knows you must return to spawn?

Do you see this dual desire in yourself?

It is natural for this part of self to feel melancholy, but that doesn't have to define you.

THE END OF WINTER

Each sign in the zodiac corresponds to a season in the year. This is one of the important ways to approach our understanding of signs.

Falling on the calendar from February 19 to March 20, Pisces represents the end of winter. Pisces is the period of time when the weather can swing between last gasps of serious cold and sneak peeks of the spring to come.

From the perspective of the northern hemisphere, the spring signs (Aries, Taurus, and Gemini) bring youthful (re-)birth energy. The temperature rises, shoots of plants and leaves and flowers reach out toward the sun, and the land seems to wake from slumber. We can ask and discover what new theme wants to move through us as we recommit to growth energy.

The summer signs (Cancer, Leo, and Virgo) bring us peak heat and the establishment and celebration of what we've been learning and growing. Summer is still youthful but more mature now. We are invigorated by play, abundance, and love. We can ask and discover how we best take care of ourselves and show up for our brightest self.

The autumn signs (Libra, Scorpio, and Sagittarius) invite us to a more inward way of being. The colder winds and shorter days bring us inside more, and the falling leaves

bring reflection and honoring around what we've lost and what matters most to us. Parts of self beckon to slough away, skins are ready to be shed, and patterns are ready to be broken. We can ask and discover how to let inessential or unhelpful relationships or other parts of self die off in order to make space for something new to grow.

The winter signs (Capricorn, Aquarius, and Pisces) invite us into our most mature and wise ways of being, in order to survive and endure, to envision the future, and make peace with the past. Whereas Capricorn and Aquarius are energies that still strive to work work work, Pisces is the end, and it wants to let go in order to dream a new dream.

Of what does Pisces dream? As I like to say: Pisces dreams of Aries. On the one hand, Pisces holds all of the melancholy of the past and, in the other hand, Pisces identifies and uplifts the ideal to be born in spring.

Thus Pisces is like an amoebic bridge between one way of being and another. It's a great time of year for reflection, dreaming, wondering, making art, brainstorming, ending things, clearing space, and forgiveness.

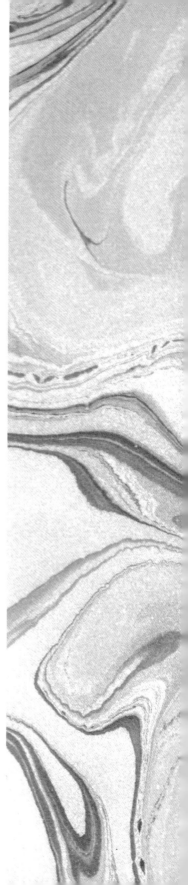

**INVENTORY OF THE
PRESENT MOMENT:
ATTUNING TO PISCES**

How do you connect with
this time of year?

What comes to mind when
you think of late February
and the first half of March?

Name some adjectives to
describe this time of year.

What makes Late Winter
beautiful?

What is the essential dignity
of this time of year? (I love
this word dignity when
applied to signs).

How do the qualities of
this time of year live in your
personality, your being,
your psyche? How are you
a "Late Winter" person?

If you don't feel that you
resonate with it, or if you
notice that you don't enjoy
or feel dislike for this time
of year, this is perfectly okay
and worth exploring!

THE 12TH HOUSE

IN AN ASTROLOGICAL CHART

In the language of astrology, a natal chart has 12 houses. Each of these represents a sphere of life or department of being human. See the Appendix to learn more.

The 1st House represents "I AM." It's your basic face, name, and identity. It's how you approach life. It's you before your conditioning. No one else exists there. In these ways, the 1st House is a lot like a baby just born into the world, letting us know who is here. The goal here is learning how to express your personal agency.

The 2nd House speaks more to the period in human development when the toddler realizes separateness and begins to claim the body, food, clothing, and toys as "mine." The 2nd House is the root system of a plant burrowing around to get what it needs from the soil in order to sustain life. The 2nd House represents "I HAVE." The goal is learning how to express your resourcefulness.

The 3rd House is associated with the part of childhood where we experience an explosion into language and a rapid development of our mental capacities. The house goes with the phrasing "I THINK." The goal is learning how to expression your clear voice.

The 4th House is related to early adolescence when we spend a lot more time in our own room trying to figure out who we are vis-à-vis the family home and how to set up our own foundations. The house goes with the phrasing "I BELONG." The goal is learning how to nurture emotional resilience.

The 5th House is concerned with discovering what we can do with our unique self-expression. It says: "I CREATE." It has to do with how we play, how we choose hobbies, and how we embody flow states.

The 6th House is concerned with the minutiae of our daily routine, health, and work patterns and dynamics. The house says: "I SERVE," because it's about how we serve our holistic well-being as well as other people.

The first six houses speak to coming into full ownership of the self. The 7th House is by analogy about the time of life when we are ready to partner. The houses can be summarized in the phrasing: "I RELATE."

The 8th House then relates to the deepening of certain key partnerships in which we merge our money, psychology, and erotic bodies. We can label this house "I MERGE." Matters of the 8th House speak to what a culture determines is taboo, in the sense that these are parts of self that we tend to keep hidden.

I use the Whole Sign system of astrology, and thus when I study charts, there is only one sign in each house. But depending on the system you used to pull up your chart, you might show 1-3 signs in your 12th House. The sign that covers the beginning of that house is the more dominant energy there.

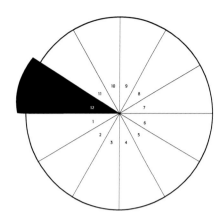

The 9th House has to do with how we expand the self through travels and mentors. 9th House affairs include higher education and living abroad – both of which force you to broaden your mind beyond the perspective of your local positionality. A keyphrase is "I LEARN."

The 10th House is the sphere of life when and how and where we test ourselves out in the public sphere. It is associated with career and public reputation. If you lived in a village, and came out in to the village square, whatever people would say about you there is what your 10th House describes. The phrase is "I ACHIEVE."

The 11th House has to do with how you constellate people together around shared hopes and dreams. It has to do with how you bring good fortune to your life based on your communities. The keyphrase is "I NETWORK."

Since the 12th House is the last of these, the 12th House resonates with endings: how we make peace, seek transcendence, and resolve the past.

The 12th House is about retreating from the material world for introspection, meditation, prayer, escaping, suffering, and exploring our inner realities. As Neptune's House, it's an oceanic space for sinking or swimming. The keyphrase is "I DREAM."

No matter how Piscean or not Piscean you feel yourself to be, you have a 12th House. We must all retreat from the world sometimes to get away, reflect, and shake off the afflictions of everyday life.

Only one in twelve people will have Pisces in the 12th House. Thus, we don't all approach our 12th House part-of-self in a Piscean way. So then how does this understanding of the 12th House help you get closer to understanding Pisces? The nature of the 12th House speaks to much of what Pisces does:

Pisces dreams.
Pisces heals.
Pisces retreats.

And most central of all: The essence of the 12th House and the essence of Pisces have to do with

YEARNING FOR INNER PEACE

When our yearning for inner peace feels impossible in the external world, when we are too heartbroken to feel it's attainable, then sometimes the 12th House comes to signify the things we do to escape our suffering.

Hence, the 12th House is often known as the House of

Self-Undoing. Part of the reason why this is so has to do with the nature of its position in the zodiac. In Living the Signs: Aries, I discuss the importance of the 1st House and how it's known as your Rising Sign. The way I read charts privileges the Rising Sign and its Ascendant degree as the point of embodiment in the chart and the key signature for giving your life momentum, direction, and actualization. The deeper you go in astrology, the more you learn about the "aspects" or mathematical relationships between planets and points in the chart. What matters to us here is the fact that our Ascendant, the AC degree, and any planets we might have in the 1st House cannot create an aspect back to the 12th House.

Hence, it's like the 12th House is "invisible" to us. Moreover, our relationship to the affairs of the 12th House do not often serve our purpose in any direct or conscious manner, and so we "self-undo" there if we aren't intentional and devoted to our relationship with those affairs.

In traditional astrology, the reason why this house is associated with everything from prison wards and mental hospitals to yoga retreats and artist's studios is because these are traditionally spaces where we go to recuperate from "the world out there."

So does this mean that if you have key placements like your Sun in the 12th House that you can't be famous or successful or productive or happy? No. Beyonce has a 12th House Sun. So does Madonna, Tony Blair, Meryl Streep, Joe Biden, Charlize Theron, Ellen Degeneres, Rihanna, and David Bowie. But when I see their charts, I know that this is a person who needs to slough off other people in order to serve their purpose in the world. Cultivating privacy and time away is simply essential for 12th House Suns (and Moon, Mercury, & Venus).

A lot of this has to do with the fact that the 12th House also relates to our connection to the collective unconscious and collective dream spaces. Strongly 12th House people can learn to access the dreams and aspirations of the collective, not to mention the people moving in and around their space. 12th House people are very porous, and able to pick up on the moods of everyone around them. This is amazing and beautiful, but it is also exhausting and confusing to take so much on in one's psyche and energetic body.

12th House Moon Greta Garbo famously declared: "I *vant* to be alone!" (In a 1955 interview, she clarified that what she said was: "I want to be let alone!") Another great example of this is 12th House Sun Richard Branson, who bought

Necker Island in the BVI as a family getaway as well as a place to host getaways for other fabulously wealthy people.

Look to your chart, if you have any personal planets in the 12th House, then some part of your life is enmeshed with the needs of this psychic space. You will serve yourself by finding regular solitude and retreat, and your purpose is likely bound in some way with healing and service, which can take many forms. You may know suffering before you figure this out.

Caroline Myss teaches us in her fascinating book *Sacred Contracts* that we each have a calling in this life. Some life-times experience more hardship and sacrifice than others. Myss teaches that some people are here to learn the skills for overcoming the burdens of the past, which they can give back to others, while some people simply don't have that contract. We waste time feeling bummed that we don't have someone else's contract.

My own chart attests to this. My Pisces Sun, Mercury, + Venus all fall in my 12th House. Until I determined to let my suffering and losses be my gift to the world instead of my sad story, I was lost. My purpose has to do with the 12th House and helping those lost in Neptune's seas find

their way back to shore. I love myself now because of my afflictions, not simply in spite of them.

Without your chart, you know intuitively right this moment how much you need alone time, retreating from the world, solitude, a space away from it all, even if it's simply a back-room space for painting or meditation. Does a quiet cabin in the woods sound like heaven to you? Is that how you come home to yourself? People resonate with that or they don't, and that's okay.

Make some time to journal about your history of retreating to solitude, and commit to more of it if you know it is part of your path to inner peace.

Whatever sign and planets you have in the 12th House will inflect the way you approach, fear, and/or need that house. These are Google-able things, though they would be most effectively parsed through in a personal reading.

INVENTORY OF THE PRESENT MOMENT: YEARNING FOR INNER PEACE

On the scale of 1 to 10, how well do you feel you
can describe yourself by the following phrases:

1 = NOT AT ALL, 10 = FULLY AND COMPLETELY

I create space away from the outside world to cultivate
inner peace.

1 ——————————————————————————— 10

I protect the well-being of my private realm.

1 ——————————————————————————— 10

I value my longing for grace and transcendance.

1 ——————————————————————————— 10

I seek forgiveness and self-forgiveness in order to
release that burden on my psyche.

1 ——————————————————————————— 10

I keep tabs on my escapist tendencies in order to transmute
them into the dreams I'm called to live.

1 ——————————————————————————— 10

I understand that my inner peace is a part of me that
only I can cultivate.

1 ——————————————————————————— 10

I commit to serving the world with what I've learned about
grief, affliction, suffering, addiction, and overwhelm.

1 ——————————————————————————— 10

*If desired, let the above statements guide you as mantras
as you work with Pisces right now.*

Commit now to answering these with gentle, loving compassion.

What does it mean to feel inner peace? How do you know it when you feel it?

When / with whom / in what situations do you feel most at peace?

When / with whom / in what situations do you decidedly NOT feel most at peace?

What does it feel like in the body to retreat from the world in small or significant ways?

What does it feel like in the body when you haven't been able to find some retreat?

What are your coping styles or habitual responses when you're feeling overwhelmed by the energies of the world?

In the coming few weeks, as you are working with Pisces, commit to noticing — with as much loving compassion and neutrality as possible — when and with whom and in what situations you feel connected to your inner peace. Commit to noticing when your body and psyche crave retreat and then give that to yourself. A regular meditation practice or a daily ritual bath are excellent ways to bring this in on the daily.

SIGN MODALITY

Pisces is Mutable

In the language of astrology, we assign three categories to describe the energy direction and movement style for each sign:

CARDINAL: starting-initiating-searching energy
FIXED: rooting-stubborn-assured energy
MUTABLE: dispersing-processing-distributing energy

These relate to where a sign falls in a season. Cardinal signs start a season, initiating the qualities of what the season will be. Fixed signs are the middle of the season, rooting into the quintessence of its energies. Mutable signs are the ends of a season, moving around and integrating all that the season was and preparing the way for the season to come.

As the end of winter, Pisces is MUTABLE. Pisces processes and integrates all that winter was and makes space for spring to come in. Wherever you are mutable, you create bridges between one thing and another:

> Gemini bridges spring to summer.
> Virgo bridges summer to fall.
> Sagittarius bridges fall to winter.
> Pisces bridges winter to spring.

The mutable signs are all 90 degrees from one another within the wheel of the year as they are within the wheel of the birth chart. The houses where you have mutable signs will indicate where you are more adaptable to change, where you welcome more options, and where you are more willing to adjust and deviate from the prior plan.

Wherever you are mutable (Gemini, Virgo, Sagittarius, Pisces), you are more flexible. You could go this way, you could go that way. You see this point of view, you see that point of view. You could choose this, or that, or some other thing.

The benefit of mutability is the ability to improvise and adapt to the environment, the relationship, and the situation at hand. The difficulty with mutability is indecision and a feeling of too many options.

Without needing to know anything
about your chart, do you feel like you
are someone with little mutability,
balanced mutability, or over-mutability?

In what areas of life (with whom / in
what situations) do you lose yourself
because you are overly flexible? When
has this been a detriment for you?

In what areas of life do you most
appreciate your flexibility and openness
to options? When has this been a gift
for you?

SIGN ORIENTATION

Pisces is Transpersonal

The zodiac is organized in a variety of ways that help us understand how each sign relates to the others. Each of these modalities brings us closer to the essence of each particular sign.

The relational category speaks to the orientation of the sign energy:

PERSONAL: focus is on self-understanding

INTERPERSONAL: focus is on being relational with the Other

TRANSPERSONAL: focus is on one's relationship to the collective

There is no hierarchy here. Personal signs are not more selfish, or less spiritually "evolved" than the Transpersonal signs. You are all twelve signs, remember? Altogether, you are whole.

The last four signs of the zodiac are transpersonal energies: Sagittarius, Capricorn, Aquarius, and Pisces. Transpersonal energies aim to understand who we are within the larger community, world, and cosmos.

The benefit of transpersonal energies is the ability to get beyond our own personal and interpersonal stories and seek a larger purpose within a grander web.

The detriment of transpersonal energies is an abandonment of the self and relationships to the world "out there."

As with everything in the language of astrology, the goal is skillful balance. Big leaders need transpersonal energy because they are giving themselves over to something larger than themselves. However, there can be an ensuing struggle to meet one's own needs and to care for the intimate relationships in their life.

In what parts of your life do you feel
most called to give and serve the
collective?

Where does your focus tend to fall on
the spectrum between personal, interpersonal, and transpersonal energies?

Do you ever abandon yourself to the
needs of the community, the public
sphere, the world?

What are some concrete ways you
could create more balance here?

WATER

*Another way we organize the zodiac is
by dividing it into four elements:*

FIRE:
our creativity, zestiness, inspiration, ecstasy, vitality, bravado, adventurousness

EARTH:
our steadfastness, stability, practicality, sensuality, structure

AIR:
our meaning-making, communication, ideas, relationality, mental frameworks

WATER:
our emotionality, intuition, feelings, instincts, inner worlds

Pisces is the third water sign after Cancer and Scorpio, respectively. The watery parts of self are more mysterious, and often operate within us unconsciously, even though they underlie most of our motivations and behaviors. Our water is our tears, our fluids, our dreams, our deep knowing, our tenderness, our most primordial, infinite, and primal parts of self. Our water is the part of us that intuitively feels the energy in a room, of a person, of anything. It is the part of us that is psychic.

The benefit of being watery is a deep attunement to your emotional, psychological, and dreaming life. By connecting authentically with yourself this way, you are able to identify and release emotional blockages. Likewise, you are able to care for others and nurture their own feelings.

The detriment of being watery is filtering all of your experience through your feelings and struggling to stay anchored with the rolling waves of emotions. You may identify too strongly with the feeling states of others and lack boundaries for your own self-care, resulting in depletion.

Let's get honest: How are your boundaries with other people?

Cancer is Personal Cardinal Water: energy that initiates personal belonging and nurturing. Scorpio is Interpersonal Fixed Water: energy that consolidates deep feelings between people. Pisces is Transpersonal Mutable Water: energy that flows, adapts, and feels beyond the self.

You use your Water signs differently, but they all speak to your overall feeling capacity and the desire to work with the nonverbal and nonvisual, but still very real, aspects of

PISCES IS MUTABLE TRANSPERSONAL WATER

human reality. Ideally, you move your Water around from one sign to the next:

The Cancer in you extends your psychic feelers into the environment to regulate a safe emotional space. The Scorpio in you plunges all the way into the most hidden places two people can share with each other. The Pisces in you feels into the collective dream in order to imagine a path for Universal Love.

Since Pisces is both Mutable AND Water, it is the most adaptable, shapeshifting sign energy. The Pisces in you can frankly be anything to anyone anywhere.

Skillful Pisces recognizes this, and creates conscious channels for direction, anchoring, and self-monitoring to avoid feeling too vast, spread out, pleasing and caring for too many people. Shapeshifting is only useful if it's supporting the anchored purpose of your Pisces.

This, dear reader, is the story of how I came back home to myself. As a Pisces Sun, Mercury, & Venus, I was like butter spread out over too much bread, because I was lost in an ocean of beautiful possibilities with no clear plan, values, or purpose. I looked to the people I admired in my life to tell me who to be.

If this is you, please take some space at the back of the workbook to write and write and write about the story of your vastness, and to vision how you want to swim back to your own sweet shores. If this is you, you will deeply benefit from this work of clarifying your Piscean gifts while also strengthening your grounding – anchoring – boundary practices.

INVENTORY OF THE PRESENT MOMENT: YOUR WATER

What is your relationship to
your feelings?

How easily or not easily do
you cry?

How strongly do you feel the
emotional states of other people?

How were your boundaries with
other people growing up, especially with your caregivers and best
friends? Did you tend to be wide
open or closed off?

What were the similarities and dif-
ferences between your boundary
styles at around age 8 and around
age 15?

How are your boundaries now?
Do you tend to be wide open or
closed off?

With whom or with what (food,
work, alcohol, shopping) do you
struggle with boundaries?

SYMBOL FOR PISCES

The Fish

The constellation Pisces shows two lines emerging from a single point, like a V, with two oval formations seemingly leaping from both ends. The Babylonians saw it as a pair of fish joined by a cord. The name Pisces is a Latin plural form of Fish. The constellation is usually associated with the Roman myth of Venus and Cupid, who tied themselves with a rope and transformed into fish to escape the monster Typhon.

Pisces is the part of us deeply connected to the collective feeling, the communal unconscious, to mysticism, to the mysteries of multi-dimensional knowing.

Channeled into skillful purpose, Pisces is infinite imagination, playful flexibility, shifting and regenerating again and again with endings and beginnings. It is the desire to connect into the infinite to find a dream, and then the will to see that dream unfold in reality. Pisces is a deep well of empathy and the ability to channel feeling into song, poetry, dance, music, healing, and other forms of intuitive communication in service to the world.

All possibilities exist for the Piscean once the dream has been identified and the Piscean wills that dream into reality!

Because Pisces understands that endings are part of life, it is an energy that accepts non-attachment. Skillful Pisces is able to grieve endings and then move on, bouncing back much more quickly than other sign energies can handle. Unskillful Pisces is over-sacrificing, addicted to suffering, and prone to escaping the harshness of life with screens, drugs, and alcohol.

Transpersonal Mutable Water isn't exactly a skillset that's encouraged and educated by our culture, so we're not taught what to do with our Pisces or how to work with it skillfully. Pisces is so open, so giving, so empathic, so shifting, by nature – it can be hard to return to the self, to find ground, to dig into anything at all.

The essence of skillful Pisces is this: living the dream you want to see in the world.

This part of you must be free to adapt, shift, and move on, so you need these two skills:
    -boundaries with your escapist tendencies
    -boundaries with over-caretaking others

If you have these, you protect yourself from falling into the trap of victimhood, martyr-dom, and suffering that is unskillful Pisces at play. These are tools that can be learned and practiced.

Have you ever read Langston Hughes' poem "Harlem?" It's a piece of writing that spoke directly to my 14-year old Piscean heart and I've never forgotten its message.

Harlem
By Langston Hughes

What happens to a dream deferred?

Does it dry up
Like a raisin in the sun?
Or fester like a sore—
And then run?
Does it stink like rotten meat?
Or crust and sugar over—
Like a syrupy sweet?

Maybe it just sags
Like a heavy load.

Or does it explode?

INVENTORY OF THE
PRESENT MOMENT:
DREAM JOURNALING

List a dream you wanted for your
life at ages 8, 12, 16, 22, 30, and
on, as relevant to your current age.

What happened to these
"dreams deferred?"
Why did you defer them?

*Circle any of the dreams that
signal melancholy or wistfulness in the body when you
think about them now.*

What can you do right now to invite in more of your dreams, not to escape but to make them your reality?

This will mean having to face the parts of your life that aren't living up to your attuned aesthetic sensibilities and desire for universal love. This will mean accepting the harshness of the world and determining not to let it smother your glorious spirit.

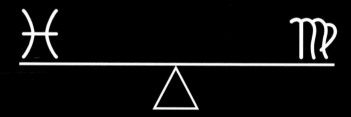

LIVING THE SIGNS

BALANCING PISCES
WITH VIRGO

The zodiac is a form of sacred geometry. Each sign has a unique relationship with the others based on their positioning and angles within the wheel. Opposing signs – the signs opposite each other – teach each other balance. Thus, whatever sign is opposite your Sun sign will help you to more wisely and skillfully live your Sun.

All Water signs are opposite Earth signs. Isn't that beautiful? Because Water, without a container, can be too vast, shapeless, directionless. Water craves a container. Water needs structure to become powerful: the curl of the surf, a waterfall, a whirlpool, an aqueduct, fluids pouring from vessels.

Together, the Earth signs (Taurus, Virgo, and Capricorn) represent the parts of self that help you with practicality, structure, organization, stability, cleanliness, reliability, and achievement.

Your Pisces is so beautiful, so special, so empathic, but without boundaries and without grounding, you will feel vast, and out to sea, and unable to keep up with the day to day. Virgo is the antidote.

Virgo is about the time of the year when pre-industrial cultures would cultivate the harvest, survey what has been done, judge what will be most needed, eliminate the inessential, and purify for the good of the community. Virgo is the part of us that discriminates and serves in honor of the self and the collective. Virgo wants it just right, for our greatest good. Virgo speaks to us of hands that whittle away at wood or shape clay to create the perfect form for us all to enjoy.

Where Pisces is about the infinite, Virgo is about the fine details. The spirit / the mind. Floating on water / hands on wood. Stream of consciousness poetry / the perfectly modulated argument. The creative process / the daily ritual.

BALANCING PISCES WITH VIRGO

With every Full Moon, the Moon is in the sign opposite where the Sun is. Thus, when we're in Pisces season, we have a Full Moon in Virgo. And likewise, the only Full Moon in Virgo in the year happens when we're in Pisces season.

Working with the Moon is a vital way to live the signs and embody the language of astrology. This is a huge part of what I teach. Turn to the activities for the Full Moon in Virgo or Pisces when you're in those seasons, respectively.

That said, every single day you can invite your Virgo to support your Pisces, and vice versa.

Circle the skillful and unskillful Virgo adjectives below that other people would employ to describe you.

Then star the ones that you would use to describe yourself.

Discriminating	Probing	Devoted	Nit-Picky
Perfecting	Problem-Solving	Humble	Organized
Purifying	Technical	Analytical	Economical
Skeptical	Healing	Conscientious	Helpful
Detail-Oriented	Judgmental	Critical	Health-conscious
Dexterous	Fastidious	Fault-Finding	Patient
Practical	Efficient	Savior-complex	Hard-on-self
Serving	Self-denying	Orderly	Petty

If you need more Virgo in your life (like I do), you can fall in love with one (as I have) to help you balance. Ha! But alas, to live the signs we must also embody them ourselves. Here are some daily Virgo activities that have helped me ground my Pisces:

- Cleaning the counter tops and everything in the sink after every meal
- Clearing out the car on a regular basis
- Keeping tidy accounting
- Thinking ahead through the next steps
- Eliminating the inessential in everything
- Pre-planning for your future self
- Problem-solving how to do things more economically and efficiently
- Noticing what other people need and showing up for them if they ask for it
- Whittling away at dreams, visions, ideas, and processes to get to the ideal form
- Monitoring and caring for one's nutritional and holistic health
- Tinkering as play
- A devotion to the details of things
- Meeting yourself at your high standards

If your Piscean tendencies lead you into clutter, disorganization, lack of follow-through, and other forms of submerged Water symptoms (raising my hand in compassion!), then committing to a few of these every morning until they become a part of your process would be highly beneficial.

I think I used to believe that these practices were "beneath" me. This is a common mistaken belief that whatever is material is more "base," and that what is spiritual is "above." Now I see how my material life serves my dreams and my goals symbiotically.

On the other hand, if you tend toward strong Virgo, if you lack Pisces, you may hold a belief that your spiritual dream life is a waste of time, or you may fear that you'll lose your efficiency if you let yourself expand into your Piscean imagination. You may have been told that from a parent. I cannot emphasize enough that a balanced life means holding both tendencies in a loving embrace. This goes for all opposing signs in the zodiac.

Are you more Pisces or more Virgo?

How do you demonstrate a balance of these energies? How are you imbalanced?

THE
PLANETARY
ARCHETYPE
FOR
PISCES

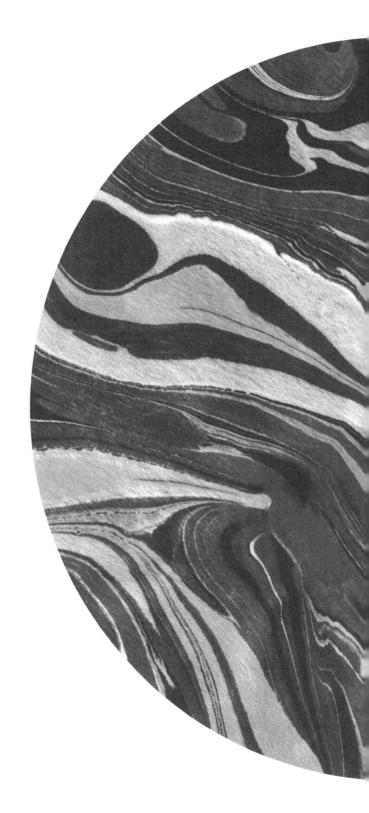

In
the language of
astrology, each sign is
"ruled by" at least one planet
and has another planet that is "exalted in" that sign. The planets represent
symbolic, archetypal energies, meaning
timeless thought-forms that we all inherently
understand no matter where or when we lived
across the human timeline.

Examples of an archetype include The Elder, The
Mother, The Hero, The Mystic, The Lover, and so on.
Each planet teaches us as a symbolic archetype, and has a
set of lessons for us to learn in this life.

The signs then are given their unique properties and qualities
by their ruling planets. The signs describe the energy of how
we do things in a symbolic way, reflecting the nature of their
ruler(s). The rulers oversee the health of the sign in a person.

Pisces is traditionally ruled by Jupiter and, since its discovery in
the 19th century, it is also ruled by Neptune. Attuning to both
of these will help us get closer to understanding the nature of
Pisces.

We also say that Venus is "exalted" in Pisces, meaning that
it is treated as an honored guest and especially welcome
in the sign. This is because Venus is deeply attuned to
Pisces, even though it doesn't rule it. Understanding
how Venus relates to Pisces thus also deepens our
relationship to Piscean energy.

If your natal chart has Jupiter, Neptune, or
Venus in Pisces, you have been given a
fortuitous and fortifying gift from the
heavens!

JUPITER

**TRADITIONAL
RULER OF PISCES**

Richard Tarnas, in his magnificent *Cosmos & Psyche*, lists the archetypal energies for Jupiter thusly:

> "Jupiter: the principle of expansion, magnitude, growth, elevation, superiority; the capacity and impulse to enlarge and grow, to ascend and progress, to improve and magnify, to incorporate that which is external, to make greater wholes, to inflate; to experience success, honor, achievement, plenitude, abundance, prodigality, excess, surfeit; the capacity and inclination towards magnanimity, optimism, enthusiasm, exuberance, joy, joviality, liberality, breadth of experience, philosophical and cultural aspiration, comprehensiveness and largeness of vision, pride, arrogance, aggrandizement, extravagance; fecundity, fortune, and providence; Zeus, the king of the Olympian gods."

When I teach about Jupiter, I lead, like Tarnas, with the idea of expansion. Think about how big Jupiter is as a planet. It's enormous! We start there. Jupiter is the idea of expanding, reaching, stretching, and growing. Jupiter is more. Jupiter is extra. Jupiter consumes as it gets bigger.

Since Jupiter is the part of us that wants more of something, it tends toward enthusiasm. "This is fun. Let's do it

some more." And in that upbeat attitude, there is buoyancy and joviality. Astrologer Debra Silverman says Jupiter is "the Santa Claus of the planets," because of these qualities. Let that image fill your sense for the archetype we're talking about here. Ho-Ho-Ho!

Like water spilling out across a surface, shifting and noodling into and under every crevice and around every corner, Jupiter gives Pisces its will to expand toward and attune to the whole of life, even the unseen, the mysterious, and the magical.

Jupiter is an inherently curious, optimistic, and enthusiastic teacher, and it bestows on Pisces its dreaming, hoping, and trusting nature. Jupiter has instructed the Pisces in us to believe in love and oneness with all things. Jupiter urges Pisces to see the beautiful in everyone and everything, which gives the Pisces in us a deep well of compassion.

In Vedic astrology, Jupiter is Guru, a word we associate with the term "teacher," because Jupiter is the planet of learning and wisdom. The quintessential Jupiterian question for me is this:

What have I been learning?

You may notice that, as a very Jupiterian person, pretty much everything I do is grounded in the idea of helping myself and helping others identify what they've been learning. Because if you know what you've been learning, then you know what skills and tools you've been developing. And if you know your tools and skills, then you understand and appreciate what makes you unique when opportunities (a Jupiter term) show up that require precisely the skills and tools that you've developed.

What does oneness look like to
you? Can you trust in it?

How do you attune to what is
non-rational, unseen, mysterious, and magical?

JUPITER IN YOUR CHART

In the chart, I have personally found the sign where someone has Jupiter tends to be an energy the person vibrates strongly, whether they know it or not, or whether or not they have other planets there. Note the sign where you have Jupiter, and consider your relationship to its needs and significations. See Appendix to help you.

The house where you have Jupiter will be an area of life where the affairs seem to come easily to you, and/or where you may feel abundant or privileged in some way. It might be an area of life where you have "no filter," as in that it might feel hard to turn yourself off to the concerns of that house because you can't ever be quite satisfied with what you have there.

In The Twelve Houses, Howard Sasportas says: "...the house in the chart containing Jupiter is an area of life in which we require a great deal of room to grow and explore. It is where we are not content with that which is routine or humdrum, but rather where we are propelled to experience life more fully and completely... As you might imagine, problems in Jupiter's house stem from overextending ourselves in that area... The planet Jupiter represents the symbol-making capacity of the psyche and we normally imbue the events and experience of the house Jupiter is in with great significance."

Jupiter rules both Sagittarius and Pisces.

So if you are a Sagittarius or Pisces Sun or Moon, then Jupiter "rules" these important planets in your chart. You want to look at the houses where you have each: Sag, Pisces, and Jupiter, and consider how stories and experiences from your life relate to the affairs of those houses in terms of your inner Jupiter.

If you are a Sag or Pisces Rising, then Jupiter is your "chart ruler," and thus working with this archetype is central to the underlying motivations of your path. Wherever you have Jupiter in your chart is where you will journey toward self-development. Your work with Jupiter is what will give your purpose both momentum and direction. This is nice to know!

If you have Jupiter right next to or creating a direct line / angle to another planet, then the qualities and principles of that planet expand as their significations become more Jupiterian, as in: much bigger.

Even if you have none of these relationships to Jupiter in your chart, you still have Jupiter in your chart because Jupiter was watching over you from the sky when you were born. And you also still have Jupiter's ruling signs: Sag and Pisces.

 In my chart, I have Jupiter in Gemini. It's my only planet in Gemini, but with Jupiter there, I have a lot of Gemini vibes. I'm very mental and interested in and curious about a lot of different things. Jupiter is in my 3rd House: I was very good in secondary school, I am lucky in siblings, I communicate and teach in my fields of interest, and I feel exuberant when I love my neighborhood.

These are all 3rd House affairs. This field of my experience is crucial to my purpose and my filters for being in the world because my Sun, Mercury, and Venus are all in Pisces, which is ruled by Jupiter. So, you could say that this means my 12th House Pisces planets look to my 3rd House Jupiter for direction. Hence, my strong Air-Mercury-writer-wordsmith vibes, despite not having a personal planet in an Air sign. You can play around with this likewise if you are a Pisces or Sag Sun. Where is your Jupiter? What's the relationship between the house of your Sun and the house of your Jupiter? You will know this intuitively, not analytically. Feel your way to your own answers.

P.S. The only "wrong" answers are the fear-based ones.

P.P.S. Do you sense how Jupiterian my perspective is?

Likewise, my 3rd House is the area of life where I tend to go overboard. I am always reading ten different books and I may or may not ever finish them. I tend to enroll in more classes than I can handle at any given time. I am in love with way more podcasts than I can possibly fully process. I have "extra" when it comes to my mental pursuits. I am learning self-awareness here, but I find it difficult to put boundaries around my Jupiter.

There's something of the addict in my behavior around learning. Where Jupiter is in my chart is an area of life that feels good and safe for me, so when life feels overwhelming, when it doesn't feel safe in my body, when I don't know what else to do with myself, I go full Gemini – 3rd House with something like a compulsion. Seeing Jupiter's placement as my feel-good space helps me sit back and ask myself: "Hey babe, is there something else going on?" This may just be something I'm feeling around for in my own way, but I am curious if you feel this way, too.

My chart teaches me where to heal and re-write my story. It is precisely in this way that your chart is a road map and guide to your empowerment. It is not a grid that locks you into your struggle. The chart is not a place to project your self-doubt; it is, rather, the toolkit for your own liberation!

Please only follow or seek astrologers who help you access your chart's infinite possibilities for transformative change! Please have zero tolerance for fear-based astrology.

NEPTUNE

MODERN RULER OF PISCES

In astrology, it is believed that when a planet is discovered, we become aware of what it teaches us. Around Neptune's discovery in the sky, we saw the rise of hypnosis, mesmerism, dream theories, psychedelic drugs in the mainstream, and multiple transcendental spiritual traditions.

Neptune represents our capacity to dream, to connect to the collective unconscious, to "lift off" from the earthly plane into what feels like a higher vibration. Neptune – as Lord of the Seas – lives the world through water: intuition, dreaminess, illusion and delusion, fantasy, possibility, intuitive connectivity, and alternate states of being.

Neptune can bring us to the heights of multidimensional consciousness as well as within the densest fogs of confusion. Like all planets, Neptune is neither good nor bad. Per usual, there's a spectrum of skillfully and not skillfully working with this planet.

Neptune bestows on Pisces these skillful and not skillful aspects. Because we're talking about such a high, transpersonal vibration, the Neptune in us can struggle to stay grounded, can deny reality, and push toward escapism. Likewise, the Neptune in us can help us transcend our past pain, find grace, cultivate forgiveness, and reach for the most glorious dreams of our imagination.

It takes Neptune 164 years to work its way around the zodiac, so Neptune will only transit through a fraction of your chart in this lifetime. If you reach your early eighties, you will experience a Neptune opposition.

To me this would feel like a call to the light, an exultant phase of spiritual awakening in preparation to dissolve into all things with death. Not everyone gets there.

Many people live to their early forties though, and this is when we experience a Neptune square to our natal Neptune (that's a 90-degree angle). This period coincides with what is known as the "mid-life crisis" sometime around 41-43 years of age and it lasts about two years. The world that we have been building - our reality train - begins to suddenly look foreign, unclear, and unknowable. We ask ourselves the very Piscean questions: *"Wait... what? Wait a second... what am I doing here? How did I get here? How did this come to be my life? Where am I going?"*

Symptoms include: feeling like your life just dropped into *Alice in Wonderland*, increased drinking or using consciousness-altering substances, fantasies about a different life, idealizing another person, wishful thinking, escapism, fear that you're delusional, increased interest in spirituality, walking away from the life you've built, feelings of vulnerability, confusion, higher levels of empathy and compassion for others, curiosity to learn about healing modalities, desire for more spiritually-rich conversations with others, more awareness of your psychic sensitivity...

Another way you can go through a Neptunian period of life can be if Neptune comes upon a major planet or point in your birth chart. Neptune in your Sun, Moon, or Ascendant degree can be a very shifting couple of years when you either sink or swim with Neptune's watery influence.

As Steven Forrest notes in his book *The Inner Sky,*

> "Some call Neptunian forays meditation. Others call them prayer or meditation. Religious language is natural to Neptune, but it is not necessary. A psychologist may touch that part of consciousness and call the process self-hypnosis. A cowboy may call it staring into the campfire. The process is universal and organic... The issue is always the same: Neptune asks us to go beyond the universe of ego, hunger, and aggression without sacrificing our ability to function as a personality."

If you are born very Piscean, or you have Neptune connected to multiple planets in your chart, then you are naturally "under the influence" of Neptune, so to speak, and may struggle to stay grounded a lot of your life.

It's important to remember that Neptune is neither good nor bad; Neptune is neutral. However, Neptune sure can be confusing for people who who haven't yet the skills in how to ground themselves, set boundaries, or stay accountable when things are under Neptune's dissolving qualities. We can be compassionate with ourselves, because we've grown up in a time when these tools are not widely taught to us or encouraged. If this resonates with you, there's a lot of support throughout this workbook to guide you in working with Neptune.

From 2012 until 2026, Neptune has been moving through its home sign of Pisces. With Neptune so strong here, it's no surprise that we've seen an increase in Piscean qualities throughout culture. Yoga has become normalized in a mass way; mindfulness is now taught in elementary schools; astrology and the tarot have surged in popularity again; and it seems like everyone has a crystal collection. Therapeutic modalities have grown so much in this time. We are becoming versed in the ways that individual and collective bodies are traumatized and we yearn to heal one another.

Likewise, since 2012, we now live in and through our screens, and screens are extremely Neptunian. Screens take us out of the body, out of the room, out of time, and into another realm.

In 2021, Neptune will move between 18 and 23 degrees of Pisces. Check your chart. Do you have any planets or points in that zone? If so, they are getting a Neptune transit. If you were born March 9 - 14, then your Sun is is between 18 and 23 degrees of Pisces, and is thus receiving a two-year transit from Neptune. You may be feeling a lot of the symptoms described here, and it might be helpful to have a supporting astrological reading.

Check your natal Neptune throughout 2021. If yours is between 18 and 23 degrees of Sagittarius, you're in your Neptune square. Likewise, you will feel nourished and guided by the suggestions throughout this workbook as you aim to move through this skillfully.

INVENTORY OF THE PRESENT MOMENT: WORKING WITH NEPTUNE

Over the course of your life, what has been your relationship to your imagination? Were you allowed to cultivate it?

How do you seek to escape some of the harsh edges of reality?

What are you dreaming for your life right now in the present moment?

What limits are you placing on those dreams?

How can you gently expand those limits and make your dreams bigger, more exciting, more transcendent?

VENUS

EXALTED IN PISCES

Venus is the archetype of The Divine Feminine. Venus is for everyone, regardless of gender identification, because we all are made of both masculine and feminine energies. Venus represents your capacity to attract, magnetize, and receive what you want and desire. Venus rules the Earth sign of Taurus and the Air sign of Libra. Venus is "exalted in" Pisces, meaning that even though the planet doesn't rule the sign, it has all of its powers.

Since Venus is between you and the Sun, the archetype operates as a key filter for your human experience of purpose, power, and radiance. The symbol for Venus depicts the circle of spirit above the cross of matter, reflecting Venus's great purpose for you: to help you discover yourself through embodied experiences of love, beauty, and pleasure.

The Overculture in which we live would like us to believe that Venus is a side-teacher, a romantic interest to the hero, a pretty little ditty. What's missing here is the potent vitality and visceral generativity of this archetype. Venus is what the yoga teachers call Shakti: the primordial, cosmic energy that runs life force energy through everything, including all creation and destruction.

Venus makes things beautiful, which is why Taurus, Libra, and Pisces are often tied to artistic sensibility. The origins of "*aesthetic*" lead back to the ancient Greek aisthesis. In his book *The Thought of the Heart & the Soul of the World,* archetypal psychologist James Hillman describes aisthesis as "a breathing in or taking in of the world, the gasp, the 'aha,' the 'uh' of the breath in wonder, shock, amazement, an aesthetic response to the image (*eidolon*) presented... Images arrest. They stop us, bring us to a standstill... the flow of time is invaded by the timeless."

In my favorite book *The Speech of the Grail: A Journey towards Speaking that Heals and Transforms,* Linda Sussman discusses Aphrodite (the Greek name for Venus) as an energy present in healing speech. Sussman reminded me of Aphrodite's / Venus's origins, born of the foam of the ocean after Titans cast her father's penis into the sea. The goddess's willingness to be unclothed, displayed, revealing herself and reveling in her gorgeous nakedness, is part of her healing art.

As Sussman describes it: "Through seeing, imagining and speaking the beauty of things, just as they appear, and all the while appearing just as she or he is, the initiate-speaker [meaning anyone willing to learn to speak in a way that heals] transports self and listeners behind and beyond appearances. That is when the worlds touch, sensuously interpenetrating in Aphrodite's embrace."

Venus attunes beautifully to Pisces because Pisces is about universal love, inner peace, and the beauty of our dreams – all qualities that Venus can lovingly get behind and support. Venus in Pisces is compassion, mercy, tenderness, forgiveness, and all HEART.

A keyword for the Venusian part of Pisces is GRACE.

Venus in Pisces has the energy of the Buddhist deity Guanyin or Quan Yin. Some translations for this name include "sound perceiver" and "one who perceives the world's lamentations." Both of these suggest a deep attunement to the non-material world, with the latter specifically relating to Guanyin's perception of suffering. Thus, Guanyin is known as the ancestor or goddess of unconditional love and compassion. She is often depicted with a thousand arms and a thousand eyes so that she can sense the pleas of and care for all those who suffer.

I encourage you to take some time to learn about this goddess, who in turn teaches us about the path of the bodhisattva. In *Astrology and the Authentic Self,* Demetra George ties the bodhisattva archetype to those who have 12th House placements.

> "In Eastern doctrines, a bodhisattva is an enlightened being who consciously chooses to incarnate in order to alleviate suffering and to assist others in the search for liberation. Bodhicitta is the enlightened motivation or attitude that inspires a person to become a bodhisattva in order to benefit all beings."

In my own chart, I have Venus in Pisces. It is the only planet in my chart that holds "dignity," meaning that it's in the sign of rulership or exaltation. It is a beautiful part of my being, but it hasn't been without its "journeys" to skillful expression. I have never wanted anyone to feel bad about themselves, to the extent that I would let them run over me. I always felt guilty winning tennis matches or "beating" people in competition, so much so that I have often held

my full power back in order to give other people a chance to shine. *"I could see how much they wanted it."* That kind of behavior creates dysfunction for the ego. For years of my life, I had a habit of getting drunk with people in order for us to exult in our shared suffering. Once, deep in meditation, I asked myself why I had done this for so long, and I heard: *"How else will they know I love them and that they're not bad people?"*

The Venus in Pisces placement is a treasure. I also say this to my clients with Moon in Pisces. I've learned over time that these require deep respect and self-responsibility. The first way to begin honoring your Pisces placements is to learn compassionate boundaries as a form of protection for you and for others around you. The next thing to do is to stop engaging in any forms of aestheticizing your suffering and to own a more skillful expression of your beautiful gifts. Finally, the goal is to align with the Guanyin archetype of the bodhisattva rather than the martyr, lost bird, or victim. It is crucial to translate your Piscean gifts into forms of devotion and creativity that don't drain your spirit.

Whether or not you have Venus in Pisces, you can attune to this kind of placement and bring it into your life. Venus in Pisces is beauty expressed through compassion and love.

INVENTORY OF THE PRESENT MOMENT: CULTIVATING VENUS IN PISCES WITHIN

What does grace mean to you, in all its inflections? How and when do you embody grace?

How could you let the principle of grace infuse the cells of your body and the actions of your day a little more right now?

What does it mean to be merciful? To be compassionate? To be all-loving? How and when do you embody these qualities? What limits do you place on universal love?

What is the source of fear behind these limits? How could you let mercy, compassion, and love infuse your life a little more right now?

STORYTELLING WITH PISCES

"Sealskin, Soulskin"

Perhaps my favorite fairy tale from *Women Who Run with the Wolves* by Dr. Clarissa Pinkola-Estés is the one called "Sealskin, Soulskin," which she shares and then analyzes in a chapter titled "Homing: Returning to Oneself." I will offer it here first by memory, and then I will weave in my analysis after, as a way to attune even more to Pisces.

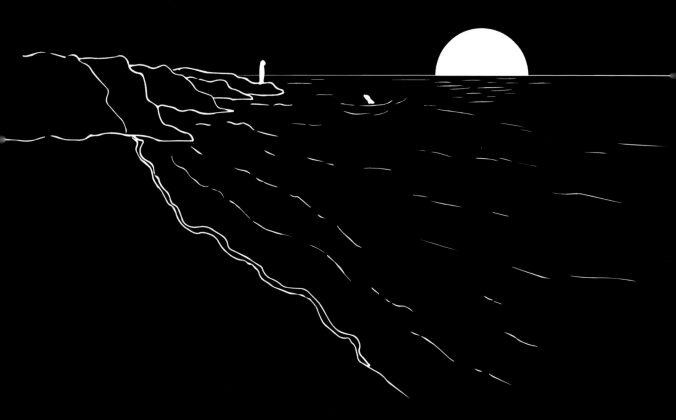

In a land up north in a time long past, a selkie (part human / part seal) was bathing onshore with her sisters one day when a kind but lonely man came upon them. He watched in wonder at the beauty of these creatures, with their deep, wise, black eyes. He noticed their sealskins set aside and before he could help himself, he swiped one and hid it in a nearby cave.

After their bath, each selkie put back on their sealskin and returned to the sea. When the last selkie couldn't find her sealskin, the old man stepped forward to help her. "I will take care of you," he said. As she had nowhere to go and no one to trust, she agreed to follow him home. The man clothed and fed her, and eventually they married. For years she lived with the man, enjoying partnership, and raising a son. She had precious things she loved, like instruments for playing music and a beautiful brush for her hair.

After some time she begins to notice her skin is sagging, her color has run out, and her eyes have no sparkle. She asks for her sealskin back, but her husband accuses her of trying to run away from them.

One night the boy awoke to a howling wind calling his name, and he followed its sounds around the shore, over rocks and crag, all the way back to the cave where his father had left his mother's sealskin. He lifted it to his face and the full force of his mother's scent poured through him in a way that felt like both joy and pain.

On his way home, his mother found him, her eyes full of shimmering gratitude to see her sealskin, and with a great heave, she reached for her skin. As begins to surround herself with its soft, wet protection, her son beseeches her not to leave him. "No Mother. No! Don't go away!," he cries. He can tell that his mother needs this in a way that is ancient and beyond his understanding.

The selkie can't bear to leave her child, and yet she knows she will die without her sealskin. So, in that moment, she brings her son into her arms, "Come me with me, my love," and with all her love, seals a protective kiss on his mouth. With that, she dives into the ocean shore, her son at her side, deep deep deep down into the water. With each swish of her tail, with every swoop of her body, she feels herself enlivened and animated once more. She has come home. With glimmering eyes, she sees clearly her family come to greet her and her son.

Many moons passed before it came time to bring her son back to shore. It was not yet his time to live with her in the seas. With all the family gathered round, she hugged him goodbye, and assured him they were always there for him. She reminded him of her instruments and her hair brush, and ensured him that any time he engaged with these, he would feel and hear her. Moreover, if he ever needed to speak to her, all he had to do was call, and she would answer.

The boy grew tall and strong. He became a wise and giving member of his community, known for his musical abilities with his mother's instruments. He was often seen at the edge of the shore, and it was said he would talk to the local seals, the ones with the deep, wise, dark eyes.

I can't talk, write, or think about that story without tearing up. It works on many levels that I aim to draw forward.

On one level, the seal represents our soul, which for a time we have to set aside in order to be practical, survive on this planet, and serve our ego. The lonely man is this part of us. Pinkola-Estés feels that the story has a "theft of treasure" motif, and speaks to the part of us that experiences some kind of rupture of innocence, or loss of selfhood, or interruption of one's dreams. As she notes, this sense of theft can come "because of naïveté, poor insight into the motives of others, inexperience in projecting what might happen in the future, not paying attention to the clues in the environment, and because fate is always weaving lessons into the weft."

The Piscean self can be blindsided because it's a part of us that trusts in the goodness and beauty of the world. The seal maiden represents that in us which is both a wild, mystical creature and also able to live and function in the human world. In our pelt, we feel fully at home in our being; we feel cohesive and whole; we hear ourselves and have our energy. We lose our soulskin when, in order to adapt to this and that loss of our sense of self, we over-align with the ego. In a world that is all go-go-go and do-do-do and be-be-be, it is quite easy to lose track of one's pelt. The lonely man inside says to the soul: "I will take care of you," and we submit in order to survive.

The son is the child of our soul and our ego, a part of us that Pinkola-Estés calls our spirit child. It is the boy who finds the pelt for his mother and returns it to her. The spirit feels and answers the call on the wind to come home. Likewise, as Pinkola-Estés offers, "The child is a spiritual power that impels us to continue our important work, to push back, change our lives, better the community, join in helping to balance the world... all by returning to home. If one wants to participate in these things, the difficult marriage between soul and ego must be made, the spirit child must be brought to life. Retrieval and return are the goals of mastery."

Have you ever had a sense that you were slowly dying to your life? That you were drying out, shriveling up, far from your magic? That you weren't sure how much longer you could keep on if you listened only to the worldly demands of your ego or of the world?

What was it that woke you up? What was the call on the wind that brought you back? What did you have to do to make a change and return home?

There are many ways we can come home in mundane and simple ways every day: zen-like activities, time alone to write about your dreams or make art, singing, walks in the woods, cooking without distraction, laying on the ground in stillness, listening to water lapping, re-reading your journal, praying, meditating, zoning out in the shower, potting plants in silence. As you may have noticed, these are all Piscean things to do... because Pisces is a sign associated with what Overculture would call "a waste of time." This. Is. So. Important. Coming home does not have to be a massive rift from your prior ego-led life, though it can be.

The spirit knows that one can only serve the world, the family, the school, the social group, or the company to the degree that one serves the soulskin. Do you hear me, you beautiful mothers, you wonderful activists, you incredible healers, you dedicated volunteers? Are you listening?

Pinkola-Estés writes:"It is right and proper that women eke out, liberate, take, make, connive to get, assert their right to go home. Home is a sustained mood or sense that allows us to experience feelings not necessarily sustained in the mundane world:

wonder, vision, peace, freedom from worry, freedom from demands, freedom from constant clacking. All of these treasures from home are meant to be cached in the psyche for later use in the topside world."

When the selkie takes her son with her under the surface of the water and they meet their extended seal family, this represents our access to our intuition, our ancestors, our spirit guides, and our most ancient, wise self. The child can't stay, however, because the child represents the way in which we are "medial beings," both wild and domesticated, destined to live our spiritual path here on the planet. We must be both mystical and embodied, dreamers and doers, seers and seekers, on the earthly plane. And thus the boy lives on, attuned to the call of the seal family while also serving the community in vital ways.

Truly, all that is needed to stay revitalized with our soulskin is the ability to tune out distractions. This is akin to what I call "closing the container" in ritual space, but it can be more simple. It's the ability to put the boundary there for a bit. And then listen, attune, replenish yourself.

This is skillful Pisces.

On another level, this story moves me in two personal ways. First, I lost my dad unexpectedly when I was sixteen, and then for a string of years after that, many unfortunate things happened to me, some heartbreaking, some traumatic, all soul loss. I was like the selkie without her skin: a sleepwalker, I moved through life, slowly dying. I was also like the boy if instead he roamed the land looking for his mom, not knowing where to find her. Lovely things happened in my life, many good times were had, things learned, places seen, but I wasn't "home" in myself.

When the boy cries "No, Mother! Don't go!" I see myself at sixteen, sensing that a part of me died, not having the cultural support to guide me through this rite of passage and retrieve myself from despair. It took over twenty years for me to learn how to dive in and find my support team, to trust and feel the deep, wild connection, and that has made all the difference.

Second, in the boy full of pain and fear that he's losing his mother, I see my younger daughter, who felt me pull away a few years ago to return home to myself after divorce. I could feel her fear that I might become a stranger to her. I see myself as the selkie, knowing that if I didn't get my skin on, I was no good to my daughters anyway. I had to dive in for a while by myself before I could understand how to bring her with me. This has been repaired, and I do believe for as long as she lives, she will know how to follow the scent of her soulskin. (My older daughter, dear Scorpio, has understood my process from the beginning, in her deep, quiet, knowing way.) If there's anything I want for my daughters it is for them to trust the call of their spirit to return home, and not to put up with people who would prevent them.

May it be clear that though in many ways my ex-husband was like the lonely man in this equation (he took care of me and we created children together), he most definitely did not steal or hide my soulskin. No one is to blame for my sleepwalking. As in all things: it takes proper timing to hear the call of the spirit.

I hope you enjoyed this story of "Sealskin, Soulskin." And I hope you remember to return home as often as possible.

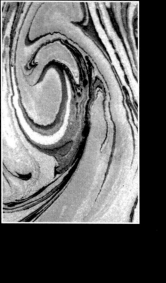

ASTROLOGY & THE TAROT

The tarot is another form of symbolic language. It is incredibly potent as a vocabulary for psycho-spiritual-intuitive awakening because it is anchored in visual form. Each of the 78 cards together represent the entirety of the human experience.

Skillful tarot artists layer each card with holographic resonance and countless possible meanings. Furthermore, the more decks you study and work with, the more layers you add to your bank of possibilities for each card.

Astrology and the tarot have long been braided by practitioners. Knowing the cards that represent each sign and planet deepens the astrologer's understanding, and learning the astrological language associated with each card helps the tarot reader broaden his or her interpretations even more.

You do not need to have any understanding of the tarot to appreciate what follows.

If you are new to or still beginning a tarot practice, see the Appendix for Tips for Starting a Tarot Practice.

TAROT FOR LIVING THE SIGNS

A Practice for Radiant Embodiment

There can be a lot of fear and even shame around approaching the tarot. Fear that it'll be really complicated to learn all of the cards. Fear that you won't be "good" at it. Fear that people will judge you for being into something metaphysical. Fear you'll feel ridiculous. Fear that it's set up for some people and not others. Fear that you'll find out about bad things that will happen to you.

If you'd like to experiment with the idea that it might be fun, helpful, inclusive, calming, presencing, and/or interesting to you, and you're feeling a Yes here, then here are some simplified suggestions for getting started. The only way to work with your fears is to go ahead and get more information.

My approach to the tarot is rooted in the soul-based perspective of my teacher Lindsay Mack. As Lindsay defines it:

> "Soul Tarot centers tarot in the present moment (rather than the past or the future), and views each card as medicine for us — not to us. It invites us to investigate and release our judgements and projections about what we've been taught about the tarot, emphasizing ethics, integrity, compassion, critical thinking, and inclusivity. It is tarot for a new consciousness, tarot for whatever arises" (*tarotforthewildsoul.com*).

From this perspective, the tarot offers us access to whatever is going on beneath the surface of our automatic experience. The tarot helps us hear ourselves. I believe the reason this happens is because the tarot is a visual and non-verbal experience, and thus each card - as image - gives us a range of options for understanding meaning and not one single answer. Within the holographic possibilities each card presents, we attune to our truth from the feel of its visual language.

This is why it is best to choose and work with a deck (or many decks) with which you feel an energetic, aesthetic resonance. The more a deck calls to you, so to speak, from the marketplace, the more clearly you'll likely hear its messages in your psyche and your body when you actually play with it.

THE BEAUTY IS THERE'S NO WRONG WAY TO SHUFFLE, TO PULL, OR TO INTERPRET THE MESSAGE

Remember that the title of this workbook series is *Living the Signs: Astrology for Radiant Embodiment*. The goal is to support you in taking what starts as mostly intellectual, abstract concepts and then bringing these into your lived human experience, so you can feel more animated by these astro-mythic-symbolic archetypes in a literal, embodied way.

Before diving in, please read through the process suggested here if you are relatively new to the tarot. In the following pages, as with all of my *Living the Signs workbooks*, I offer some formulas for tarot readings you can perform for yourself to connect with the archetypes about which we are learning.

If you don't have a deck or tarot isn't for you at this time, you can simply approach these activities like journaling prompts.

Have fun with this!

See page 140 in the Appendix for further guidance on cultivating a tarot practice.

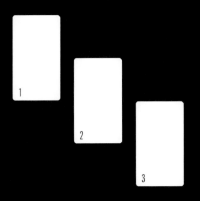

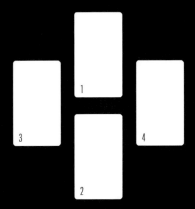

THE PROCESS

Always work with a tarot deck that you trust (see the Appendix for insight on choosing the right deck for you).

In some of these exercises you'll be meditating on the medicine of one card in particular (The Moon, for example). In that case, if you have more than one tarot deck, you can pull The Moon from another deck so that the card of focus has a chance to "participate" in the deck from which you will draw for the full reading.

Begin by feeling into the visual inspiration of the card.

Take a few deep breaths on purpose and arrive to the reading. Connect into your intuition. Ask the energy of that archetype to guide you.

Shuffle according to your unique, never-wrong style.

Center and focus your question thus:
For my highest and best, at the highest levels of love and compassion, I want to know: _____

Sit with the cards you've pulled. What you're looking for here is a message about how to connect to yourself with intuition, which means recognizing your own truth.

If you're new to the tarot, resist any initial desire to look to books or websites to give you "answers." You have the answers.

If you feel like you have received all the insight you can gather and now wish to check a guidebook, be sure that you gently question the writer and feel affinity with the interpretation before accepting it. The whole point of the tarot is to hear your own wise voice.

Open up to the yummiest possibilities for each reading. It is my personal take on the tarot that all cards are medicine and have teachings for your highest and best. Whatever cards come forward, see their most dignified and loving message for you. The Death card, 5 of Pentacles, The Tower, The Devil: if any of the "hard" cards come to you, they are here to liberate you and show you big love. Yes!

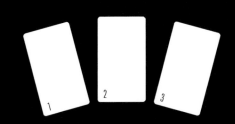

PISCES IN THE TAROT

The Moon

In the tarot, the astrological Moon is actually associated with the High Priestess card, while the Moon card is associated with Pisces. This analogy underlines the deeply intuitive and mysterious qualities of Piscean energy.

In the Smith-Rider-Waite deck, the most traditional and widely known set of cards, artist Pixie Coleman Smith depicts a large moon that seems to be both full and crescent at once. This underlines the Moon's shifting nature. In the world we live in today, change and shifts are feared.

And yet, change is reflected to us everywhere in nature – especially by the Moon – and thus the Moon card is first and foremost an invitation to own and love the parts of self that shift, roll, foam, swirl, burst, and crash like the waves and tides of the ocean that the Moon controls.

The Moon says it's okay to sometimes feel like being introverted, to sometimes feel serious, to sometimes feel melancholy, to sometimes feel anger, to sometimes feel like napping. That any phase we are in, we are always still ourselves. Just like the Moon.

Do you allow yourself to be all your phases? Have you been made to believe that you have to hold the same façade 24/7 in order to be understood, knowable, nice, and "reliable?" You may align so deeply with that belief that you may not even understand the power of this question. That's ok! How can you love your tides, your moods, your variability, and your desire for change?

Pisces is the Shapeshifter. Pisces must be free to try on guises, roles, ways of moving and speaking. Like a chameleon, Pisces wants to see what it would be like to merge into different skins.

At the bottom of the Moon card, we see a crustacean coming up out of the waters of the shoreline. Water is symbolized often in the tarot as our intuition, our inner world, our dreams, our feelings. The crustacean scuttering up the shore represents the animated life force of our dreams, aha moments, memories, intuitive feelings, spiritual guidance, and deepest knowings that can suddenly rise up and out of our unconscious realms and are made known when we are open to be in Moon time.

Moon time is akin then to the darkness of the inner life. It's hidden and mostly non-visual and non-rational. This is why we associate dance, music, painting, dreams, and oracular visions with Pisces. The possibilities of these forms of communication are hidden beneath the surface of our inner "waters," so to speak. We call them forward when we are in the Moon card. We tap into a part of self that bubbles up a vision or a movement or a vibration to our knowing, in a way that is not analytical or logical. Where it comes from is mysterious.

In the card, we also see a dog and a wolf howling to the Moon above. This pairing represents the duality between our

THE MOON.

domesticated personality and our primal nature. We are all deeply conditioned, programmed, and thus domesticated by our families, the institutions that educated us, the communities to which we assign our belongings, the rhetoric of the country we give our allegiance, and the all-pervasive media: TV, social media, movies, magazines, advertising, and so on.

The Moon card challenges you gently and lovingly to study your conditioning in the privacy of the dark. To help you, the Moon invites you to let your inner wolf be your guide.

Howl to the Moon. Let loose your wild nature. Release the aspects of domestication that have locked you in a cage. Pisces is this, too. Pisces is a mermaid diving! Pisces is a siren calling! Pisces is a jellyfish dancing!

The reason Pisces feels so much melancholy, and the reason Pisces wants to escape, and the reason Pisces zones out is because... well, it's just so incredibly depressing to be caged. And it's so sorrowful when people don't see the wonder and magic that's everywhere. And it's a downer that the world is so automated, conglomerated, and standardized – the ultimate in

The Moon card depicts two towers in the distance, inviting the viewer to move toward and through these pillars, suggesting a passage, a journey, a process.

Being "in the Moon"– which is to say, living your Pisces – is a passage to the self, and it's not for your mother, BFF, or spouse to cross with you.

That said, you can seek guides – healers, astrologers, therapists. And you can invite a witness – someone in your life who lets you be you without trying to persuade, own, or control your thoughts. If you find yourself needing validation, then you aren't really in the Moon.

How do you feel about doing solo work? Are you able to carve out time, energy, and attention for yourself and not for any kind of external validation? Have compassion with yourself if this makes you nervous. You will get there! The courage to ask these questions is the beginning of the journey!

To awaken your wild nature, I encourage you to devour Dr. Clarissa Pinkola Estés's canonical text *Women Who Run with the Wolves*. As soon as possible.

THE JOURNEY IN THE DARK IS TRULY, ULTIMATELY SOLO WORK.

INVENTORY OF THE PRESENT MOMENT: WORKING WITH THE MOON

How does it feel to read about
The Moon in the tarot?

What cages have you known in your
life? How are you still caged?

How do you tap into your wild wolf?
When do you feel most unleashed?
Who encourages you to be your most
gnarly, natural self?

What habits, personality traits, and
ways of being do you suspect or know
grow from the "domesticated" parts of
your identity and may not actually be
true to your more primal nature?

A TAROT SPREAD WITH THE MOON

Feel into the visual inspiration of The Moon.

Connect into your intuition. Ask The Moon - Pisces energy to help you with this reading.

For my highest and best, at the highest levels of love and compassion for me and all sentient beings, what is the loving invitation to connect with The Moon?

Pull 7 cards according to your own unique process of knowing with the following prompts:

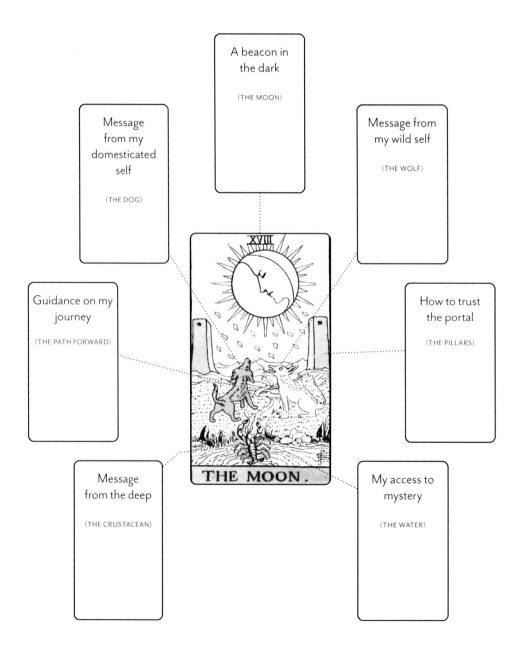

A beacon in
the dark

(THE MOON)

Message
from my
domesticated
self

(THE DOG)

Message from
my wild self

(THE WOLF)

Guidance on my
journey

(THE PATH FORWARD)

How to trust
the portal

(THE PILLARS)

Message
from the deep

(THE CRUSTACEAN)

My access to
mystery

(THE WATER)

JUPITER IN THE TAROT

Wheel of Fortune

The Wheel of Fortune is the major that I most consistently pull in my own life. This is a funny-looking card in a lot of decks, loaded with esoteric symbolism. And then there's the name, which reminds us of the long-running game show "Wheel... Of... Fortune!" Ding ding ding! Here comes Vanna White.

The game show is actually a pretty good place to start with this card. The wheel turns round and round: sometimes we lose a turn, sometimes we win big, sometimes we land safe enough. But it's not all chance. Our fortune is in part based on our general preparedness, the ability to think quickly and instinctually, and to know when and when not to take strategic risks. And the general tip: don't call out a letter somebody already tried, which basically means – pay attention.

The term Wheel of Fortune goes back to the Roman goddess Fortuna, daughter of Jupiter. Fortuna is the personification of luck. The first reference to Fortuna's "wheel" (the Rota Fortunae) is from Cicero. It was common for writers (or characters in a story) across ancient, medieval, and Renaissance times to complain about Fortuna, who blindly spins her wheel of fate, bringing some people into hard times and others into prosperity.

In old manuscripts, kings and other powerful figures were often depicted falling off the wheel in hard times, which is a visual trope often repeated in the tarot depictions of Wheel of Fortune (notably my favorite deck, the Morgan Greer). The idea goes that even the seemingly powerful and invincible among us can lose it all. We see this repeated in Death and The Tower; every king eventually dies, even Versailles could be looted by the people.

In astrology, the *Pars Fortuna*, called alternatively the Path of Fortune or Part of Fortune, represents a mathematical point in an individual's birth "wheel" derived by the longitudinal positions of the Sun, Moon, and Ascendant (Rising) point. It represents an especially beneficial point in the chart, bringing

you good things that you can't engineer yourself. Fortuna brings them to you. At *astro.com*, you can set up your search to include the Part of Fortune so you can find yours. In the Extended Chart selection, look under Additional Objects.

Life is not predictable. What at first looks very fortunate can turn into something that brings harm or despair. What initially looks unfortunate can become our most treasured learning experience. Is it even possible to say? Only the turn of the wheel will tell.

My Jupiterian grandfather had an American Dream kind of story because he was born and raised with very little financial wealth and then accumulated enough to pay for his six grandchildren's private school education and college tuitions. He was able to invest in a property on a lake in the woods for his family that still nourishes my soul every year. He took to us to many countries, skied mountains with us, and gave us many abundant meals. And yet, his wife (my grandmother) was diagnosed with MS in her late forties and he was her bedside nurse the last two decades of their lives. She couldn't dance with him or ski or explore the world with him anymore; and she couldn't eat or serve her basic needs without his help. Was he a "lucky guy" or not? Who is to say? Can anyone really ever say that about anyone?

There's a lot of symbolism in the Smith-Rider-Waite version of the card. To get into the fascinating details, I recommend the episodes covering Wheel of Fortune on the podcasts *Between the Worlds* (back when it was *Strange Magic*) and *Fortune's Wheelhouse*. What matters to me for our purposes is to consider what the core medicine of the card is so that we can bring it into our lived experience, so we can "Live the Wheel of Fortune," to play off this book's series title.

As the wheel of life turns, which it certainly will, bringing us things we cannot predict or control, the invitation of the Wheel of Fortune is to be the still point in the middle of the wheel. When the Wheel of Fortune was my Year card (add the birth month number to your birth day number and then add the sum of the numerals to the numerals of the year you're in), I was told by a well-known tarot reader that I could expect good fortune. What I found was that it was a year of ups and downs, and the biggest journey of the year was in finding the right teachers and most nourishing practices for holding myself through the waves and spins.

At the start of my Wheel of Fortune year, my state of being would be wildly contracted if lost a sub-scriber or an Instagram post failed to get attention. I'd be down for the whole day, just so triggered into unworthiness. Alternatively, if I had multiple book-ings in a day or if people shared and applauded my posts, I felt like a cosmic rainbow of joy. I would latch onto either scenario as proof of bad or good fortune and bad or good future. My insecurity was fairly valid because I was a brand-new astrologer putting myself out there in ways I'd never experienced be-fore. I didn't feel like I knew what I was doing and I felt vulnerable to imposter syndrome a lot of the time.

I realized after about nine months of this (about three months into my Wheel of Fortune year), that this business of being so fragile to external valida-tion – whether loving or disapproving! – had to stop. It was just not going to be emotionally sustainable for me. I either had to learn how to hold myself through whatever came up, or I needed to switch to a professional course that was more stable for my nervous system. But I believed in my work, and I was following the arrow of my passion, and so I sought practices to build myself up.

Let me emphasize that my goal is not only to stay neutral when I feel like I have a loss, but to be neutral when I feel like I have a win. To commit to Wheel of Fortune means to know where you are within yourself no matter what the world throws at you or invites you into.

So to me, the Wheel of Fortune is not about the wheel. I've never heard anyone share this before, but this is what I learned from living with the card: the card is about connecting to the four corner figures in the card as the unshakable foundations of who you know yourself to be. In the corners we see symbols for the four fixed signs: Taurus (Bull), Leo (Lion), Scorpio (Eagle), and Angel or Water Bearer (Aquar-ius). Whether or not you have planets in the fixed signs, everyone has all four of them in the birth chart ruling parts of our lives. Our fixed signs teach us our yes and no and how to stand firmly in who we are.

During that Wheel of Fortune year, I became aware that I had symptoms of someone who had expe-rienced a lot of narcissistic abuse. Some of these include lack of self-trust, low self-esteem, shame, self-doubt, confusion, second-guessing your ideas, and issues around unworthiness. Some of these are from repeated relationship patterns, and some came from alcoholism that developed from a lack of safety in the body as a trauma response. So, I was really into learning about new frameworks for healing and rebuilding myself.

In this time, I came across a video of Meredith Miller on YouTube where she shares her "Four Pillars of Recovery after Narcissistic Abuse." I haven't ever forgotten them. Whether or not you feel you've had narcissistic abuse in your life, her framework is really helpful for strengthening from within. They are, in Meredith's words from her online *Medium* article with the same title:

SELF-ESTEEM: "Self-esteem is about supporting yourself. It's about taking control of yourself, of your mind, of your body, of your behaviors. It's about self-perception, how you see yourself. It's also about the effect that you have on the world around you... The opposite of self-esteem will show up in self-sabotage and self-destruction."

SELF-WORTH: "Self-worth is about valuing, respecting and knowing your worth. It's you valuing yourself. It's about you respecting yourself, knowing who you are and what you're worth... The opposite of self-worth will show up in shame and unworthiness."

SELF-TRUST: "Self-trust is about knowing and believing. It's knowing yourself and believing in yourself... The opposite of self-trust shows up as self-doubt and fear."

SELF-LOVE: "Self-love is about caring and nurturing yourself. It's about treating yourself well and accepting yourself... The opposite of self-love is self-judgment and self-denial."

I love this framework, and have personally found it to be deeply nourishing to me in the rebuilding of myself from the foundations. This topic deserves a wider space to unfurl, which I actually offer in my annual summer class Soft Strength. You can learn more about Meredith Miller at *innerintegration.com*. If you are recovering from narcissistic abuse, I also highly recommend the work of Dana Morningstar at *thriveafterabuse.com* and April Harter at @narcissismrecoverycenter.

Concerning the Wheel of Fortune, I propose we integrate Meredith's framework with the fixed signs:

Self-trust (Scorpio)
Self-love (Leo)
Self-esteem (Aquarius)
Self-worth (Taurus)

When you have secure foundations in each of these pillars, you are able to "improvise, adapt, and overcome" pretty much anything, to nod to my beloved, who always says this. It has to do with staying Mutable within the structure of your Fixed self. He is a Virgo Rising, Virgo Sun, Sag Moon, and Gemini Mars-Ceres, and Pisces Vesta-Pallas. Thus, he is strong in Mutability and his words exemplify that. To me, this is the great gift of Wheel of Fortune.

A TAROT SPREAD WITH WHEEL OF FORTUNE

Feel into the visual inspiration of the card.

Connect into your intuition. Ask Wheel of Fortune – Jupiter – Pisces energy to help you with this reading.

For my highest and best, at the highest levels of love and compassion for me and all sentient beings, what is the loving invitation to connect with Wheel of Fortune?

Pull 7 cards according to your own unique process of knowing with the following prompts:

Message from my...

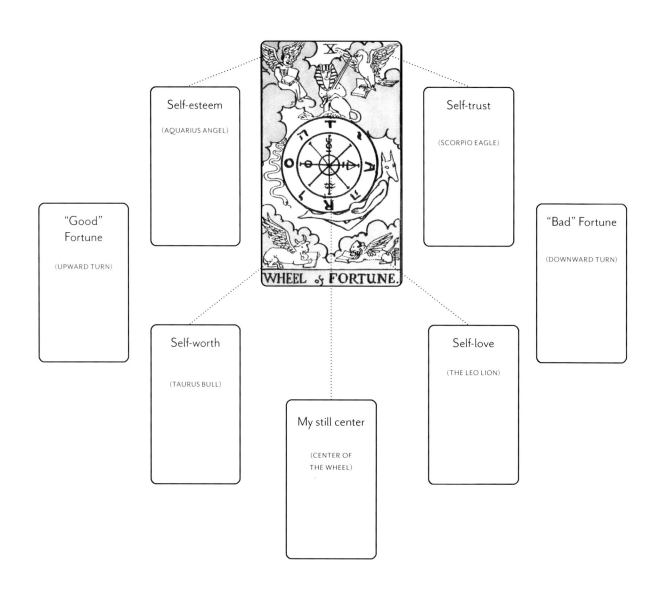

Self-esteem

(AQUARIUS ANGEL)

Self-trust

(SCORPIO EAGLE)

"Good" Fortune

(UPWARD TURN)

"Bad" Fortune

(DOWNWARD TURN)

Self-worth

(TAURUS BULL)

Self-love

(THE LEO LION)

My still center

(CENTER OF THE WHEEL)

NEPTUNE IN THE TAROT

The Hanged Man

Neptune, astrological ruler of Pisces, is tied to The Hanged Man in the tarot. Let's first clarify that the figure in this card is not "being hung," but rather, is willingly suspending themselves upside down. You can see how the figure appears relaxed, and has a halo around their head.

The Hanged Man speaks to times in your life when you have had to get a little or very uncomfortable in order to gain insight, to grow, to heal. When you know you need to invite in another perspective, another way of looking at things, something beyond your normal business as usual, even though it will require your patience and some discomfort, you are in Hanged Man energy.

It's like in yoga (and this card is sometimes called the yogi card) when you are directed to go deeper in a pose and you bump into resistance within yourself, because you don't think you can or you're afraid it will hurt, and then you do it, and there's this incredible whoosh as you open up into a release of some kind that feels cathartic. Has this happened to you before?

The Hanged Man calls to my mind the Norse god Odin, the All Father. Odin notoriously chose to hang himself upside down from the World Tree in order to seek insight and wisdom. He went without food or water, as so many mystics have done across history, in order to prove his commitment. For nine days and nine nights he waited. And then, he began to notice that the twigs and branches of the tree beneath him – that had been there all along – began to be legible as The Runes. Access to the language of the runes gave him powerful wisdom.

This is in many ways a card about initiation: of dying to be reborn. As the number 12 – like Pisces, the 12th sign – The Hanged Man can bring us back to 1 (Magician), or guide us toward 13 (Death). It is thus both a card about surrendering to endings as much as inviting in new beginnings.

The degree to which this is difficult or painful has everything to do with how strongly we hold onto our ego's attachments.

In the language of the Tarot, The Hanged Man is the willingness to surrender to the work of healing and living with clear eyes – The Hanged Man ushers us to and through the portal of a soul-centered life.

A TAROT SPREAD WITH THE HANGED MAN

Feel into the visual
inspiration of the card.

Connect into your intuition.
Ask The Fool – Piscean
energy to help you with
this reading.

*For my highest and best, at
the highest levels of love and
compassion for me and all
sentient beings, what is the
loving invitation to connect
with The Fool?*

Pull 6 cards according to
your own unique process
of knowing with the
following prompts:

Questions for the spread

FEET:
1. What/where is your
ego attaching too tightly
right now?

BODY:
2. What is the discomfort?
3. What is the story from
the past you need to see?
4. What must be
surrendered?
5. How will you do this?

HALO:
6. What is the gift of insight?

FEET

BODY

HALO

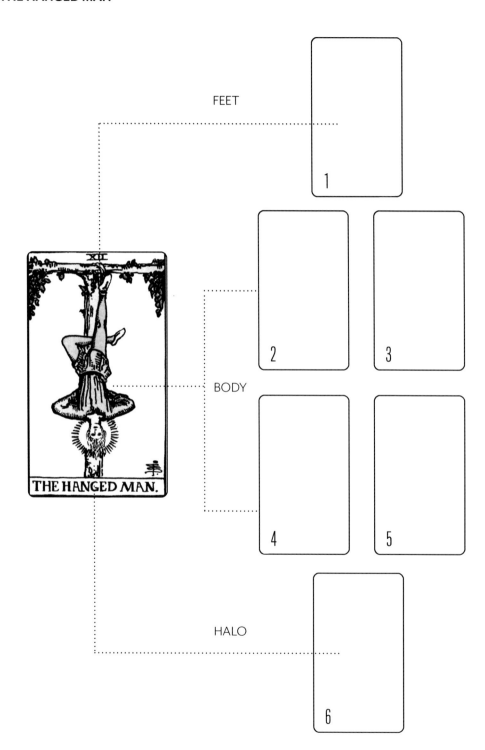

1

2

3

4

5

6

Are you willing to be patient with
The Hanged Man in yourself?

Are you willing to die to some
version of yourself from the past,
the present, or your
attachment about the future, in
order to live a more soulful life?

Write down some ways that you
are already doing Hanged Man.
What is your intimacy with the
teachings of this card?

How can you invite in more
Hanged Man to your life
right now?

PISCES IN THE TAROT

The Queen of Cups

While there is more or less consensus when it comes to the astrological associations to the cards of the major arcana of the tarot (cards like The Moon and The Hanged Man, which don't clearly identify with one of four suits), the minor arcana have more debatable, interpretive, and intuitive alignments with astrology. It's really up to the beholder, which is not a problem for me.

Within the court cards of the minors, there may be debate about which card works best for Pisces. For me, it is the Queen of Cups. All Queens are aligned with the element of Water in the tarot, so Queen of Cups represents Water of Water. Likewise, Pisces is Mutable Water, the most slippery of the signs.

In the Smith-Rider-Waite deck, we see a woman who is zoning out the external world, in profound attunement to her Cup. In French, the word *profond* means both literally deep (as in the depths of the ocean) and psychologically deep (as in intensely wise and meaningful). The Queen of Cups can go down, down, down. Down into the depths of her ancient, wise, connected knowing.

To me, the Queen of Cups has to do with deeply connecting to your inner realms of resource. Imagine how going under water removes the noise and clatter of the world above the surface. Suddenly, everything fades away and you can be with yourself. When Queen of Cups comes calling, it's time to go into your own dark caverns and find treasure; it is not a time to get a second opinion, make plans, or stay busy. Within dream, trance, channeling, or Zen states, the Queen of Cups finds everything she needs.

I first heard from Lindsay Mack how this card connects with the story "Sealskin / Soulskin" from Dr. Clarissa Pinkola-Estés' *Women Who Run with the Wolves*. You can read about this story, and how it relates to Pisces on page 68.

This card as your soulskin completely resonates for me. And there is nothing so necessary to the Piscean part of who you are than to come home. (This is also good medicine for the other Water signs Cancer and Scorpio as well as for all of the Cups in the tarot.)

A basic, daily practice for "homing," to invoke Pinkola-Estés's phrasing, is to first clear

your energy field, chakras, and emotional body of other people's energy. You attune to yourself, and then request to remove all energies or cords (claims) from other people and their energy. You sense or see this happen but it's honestly enough to just visualize and trust that it will happen if you command it.

Next, attune to your energy and call it home from wherever it's been. See your energy come back to you on a golden web, bringing all of yourself back home to you. See all of your energy collect at the top of your head as gold light, and bring it down through your crown chakra and down through all parts of your body until you are re-lit with your own energetic light.

Say: *"All of me inside of me. All of me inside of me. All of me inside of me."*

If this is foreign to you, I invite you to experiment with trying this out three times a day for a few weeks. It only takes a few minutes. This is especially important if you live with or regularly interact with someone who pulls a lot from you.

A TAROT SPREAD WITH QUEEN OF CUPS

Feel into the visual inspiration of the card you most love for Queen of Cups.

Connect into your intuition. Ask Queen of Cups - Pisces energy to help you with this reading.

For my highest and best, at the highest levels of love and compassion for me and all sentient beings, what is the loving invitation to connect with Queen of Cups?

Pull 7 cards according to your own unique process of knowing with the following prompts:

A message about...

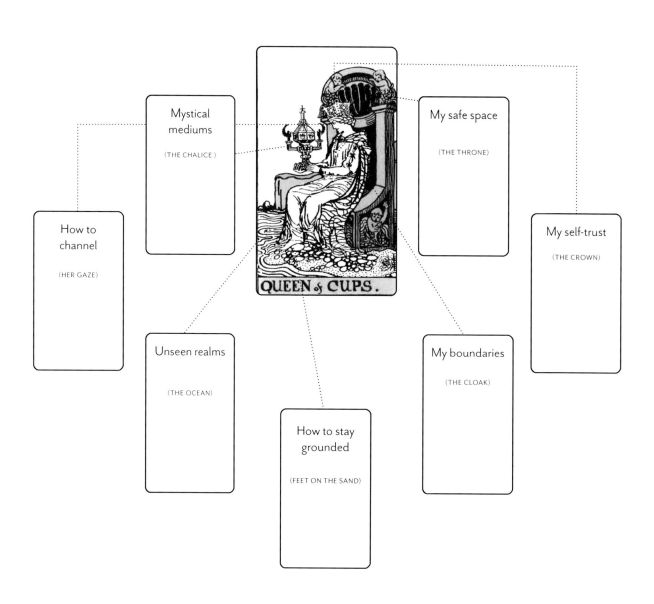

How to channel

(HER GAZE)

Mystical mediums

(THE CHALICE)

My safe space

(THE THRONE)

My self-trust

(THE CROWN)

Unseen realms

(THE OCEAN)

My boundaries

(THE CLOAK)

How to stay grounded

(FEET ON THE SAND)

CARD-A-DAY TAROT RITUAL

EXAMPLE:

☽ ♈ 2/ 19

VIII

Strength

1

Keywords:

Finding strength, the undefended heart.

Thoughts:

Feeling empowered to approach my creativity more courageously.

Working with the tarot as a card-a-day ritual for a month is incredibly stabilizing and anchoring. It offsets the high degree to which we're care-taking everything but our inner worlds. If you are looking to have more internal alignment generally, then committing to a card-a-day practice for a period of time – like committing to any healthy daily practice – will support you.

Whether you are brand new to the tarot or already in deep relationship, I invite you to pull one single card every day with a leading question of your choice. If you would prefer not to work with the tarot, you can work with a single question as a journaling prompt each morning as an act of disciplined devotion.

Here are some suggestions for working with Pisces themes:

Today, what is the invitation...

for re-alignment today?

to dream?

for imagination today?

to let in more love today?

to shine today?

for devotion today?

to take up more space today?

Use the following pages to track this.

Simply write the name of the card you pulled, a few related keywords you choose for calling in alignment that day, and a handful of words to note before bedtime to capture how it went working with that card all day. You might also like to add the glyph for the sign the moon is in that day as well as the date.

By the end of the cycle, you will feel more aligned because of this practice, with the added bonus that you will have a much deeper relationship to your cards.

Start with the first one now. Let's say you pulled the Strength card. Write the name of the card inside the box for that day of the lunar cycle, note the keywords for the card, and then later on note the effects of working with the card for the day.

Infuse yourself with the energy of your intention, commitment, and self-esteem.

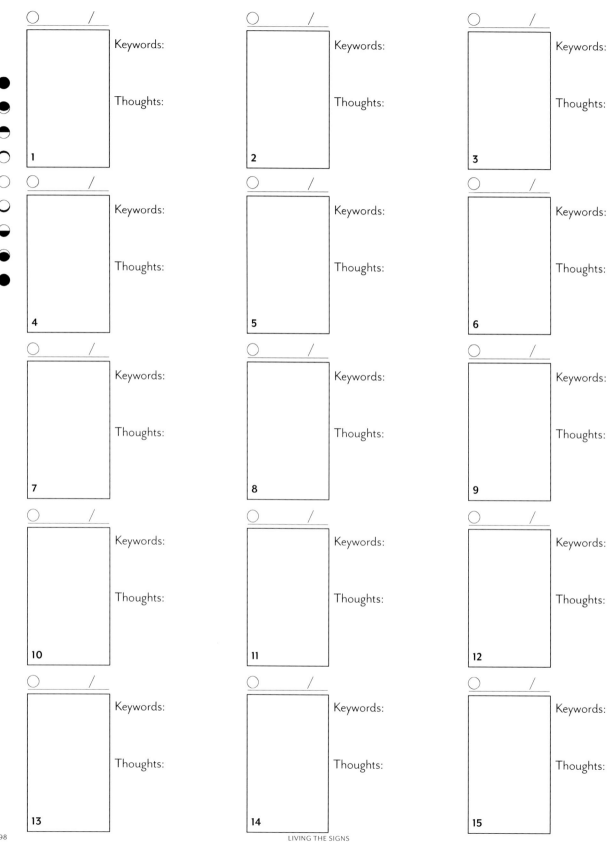

◯ _____ / _____

Keywords:

Thoughts:

1

◯ _____ / _____

Keywords:

Thoughts:

2

◯ _____ / _____

Keywords:

Thoughts:

3

◯ _____ / _____

Keywords:

Thoughts:

4

◯ _____ / _____

Keywords:

Thoughts:

5

◯ _____ / _____

Keywords:

Thoughts:

6

◯ _____ / _____

Keywords:

Thoughts:

7

◯ _____ / _____

Keywords:

Thoughts:

8

◯ _____ / _____

Keywords:

Thoughts:

9

◯ _____ / _____

Keywords:

Thoughts:

10

◯ _____ / _____

Keywords:

Thoughts:

11

◯ _____ / _____

Keywords:

Thoughts:

12

◯ _____ / _____

Keywords:

Thoughts:

13

◯ _____ / _____

Keywords:

Thoughts:

14

◯ _____ / _____

Keywords:

Thoughts:

15

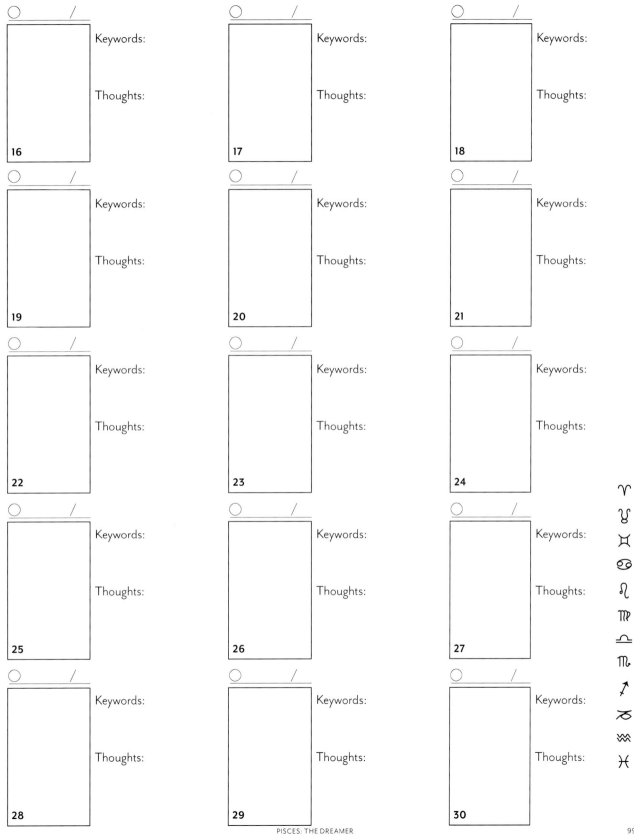

◯ ___ / ___

16 — Keywords: / Thoughts:

◯ ___ / ___

17 — Keywords: / Thoughts:

◯ ___ / ___

18 — Keywords: / Thoughts:

◯ ___ / ___

19 — Keywords: / Thoughts:

◯ ___ / ___

20 — Keywords: / Thoughts:

◯ ___ / ___

21 — Keywords: / Thoughts:

◯ ___ / ___

22 — Keywords: / Thoughts:

◯ ___ / ___

23 — Keywords: / Thoughts:

◯ ___ / ___

24 — Keywords: / Thoughts:

◯ ___ / ___

25 — Keywords: / Thoughts:

◯ ___ / ___

26 — Keywords: / Thoughts:

◯ ___ / ___

27 — Keywords: / Thoughts:

◯ ___ / ___

28 — Keywords: / Thoughts:

◯ ___ / ___

29 — Keywords: / Thoughts:

◯ ___ / ___

30 — Keywords: / Thoughts:

♈ ♉ ♊ ♋ ♌ ♍ ♎ ♏ ♐ ♑ ♒ ♓

What are you noticing?
What themes seem to be emerging?

Tally how many cards came forward
for each Minor Arcana Element:
Any repeating cards?

WANDS

SWORDS

PENTACLES

CUPS

NOTES ON WEEK 2:

What are you noticing?
How is the story evolving?

Tally how many cards came forward
for each Minor Arcana Element:
Any repeating cards?

WANDS

SWORDS

PENTACLES

CUPS

NOTES ON WEEK 3:

Tally how many cards came forward
for each Minor Arcana Element:
Any repeating cards?

What are you noticing?
What insights are trying to come through?

WANDS

SWORDS

PENTACLES

CUPS

NOTES ON WEEK 4:

Tally how many cards came forward
for each Minor Arcana Element:
Any repeating cards?

What are you noticing?
What gifts came through to you here at the end?
What did you learn this cycle?

WANDS

SWORDS

PENTACLES

CUPS

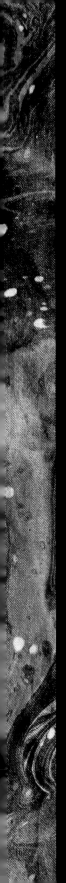

START A
DREAM
JOURNAL

In back of this workbook, or in a journal of your choice, please track your dreams as soon as you wake up in the morning. Even before you make coffee or check email or anything. Otherwise, you may lose details.

Being in positive relationship with Pisces means opening ourselves up to more dream time. Pisces is an invitation to
Be. In. Dreams.

Ideally, you have the date and then a few lines to jot down notes. To keep it from being daunting or time-consuming, give yourself permission to just write keywords or draw evocative images instead of full paragraphs. Logic and grammar are not important for this exercise.

If you are interested in working with an expert in dream interpretation, I recommend Shon MonDragon at *depthspecialist.com*

Enjoy!

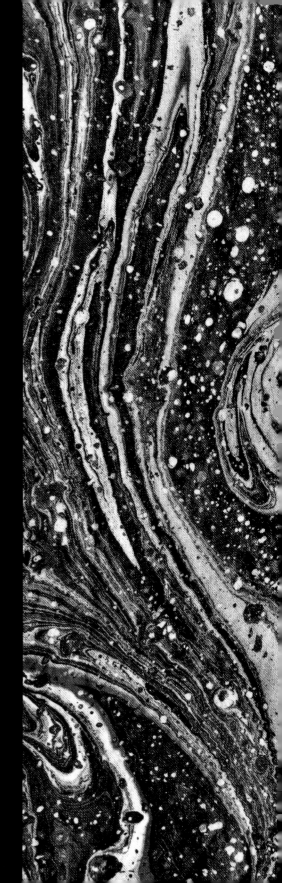

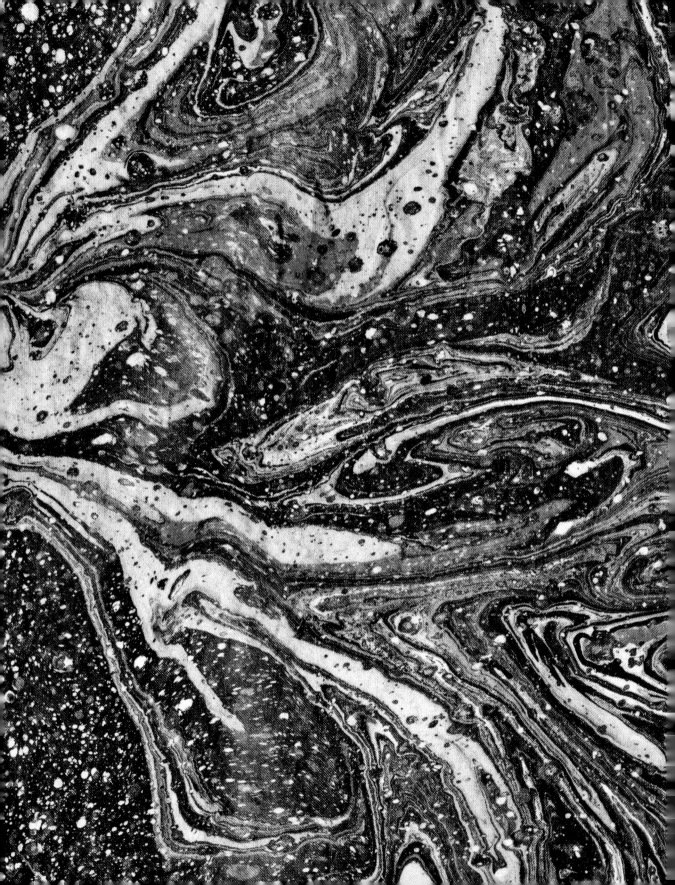

Dear Pisces,

I pledge to accept you as you are. You don't have to shapeshift to please me.

I honor your Yes and your No. I will not guilt trip you if you need your space right now.

I respect your alone time and your solitude. Take as much as you need. I will not make you feel bad about it, even if I don't understand.

I cherish your capacity to dream. I won't judge you for tuning out. I won't criticize you and tell you it's all a waste of time. I know that your visions will make the world more beautiful.

I will help you stay on task to make sure you don't get lost. I will show you how to set timers, use a planner, make lists, and organize your life so that you give a container of practicality to your watery gifts.

I will honor your boundaries. I will not take advantage of your empathy. I will not ask you to lose yourself by taking care of me.

I will be patient with you if you are suffering. I will encourage you not to give up on your dreams. I will not judge you in periods of escape and affliction. I will not take pleasure in or enable your self-destruction.

I will allow you to be as big and bright and beautiful as a shining star. I will not feel envious, because I know that if you sense I feel bad about myself that you will shrink your light in order to help me feel better, and I won't ask that of you.

I will not encourage you to walk into a lion's den of toxic energy even if it's what our culture says is popular or cool or powerful.

I will accept that you are adaptable and able to move on much more quickly than most. I won't take it personally if you bounce back more swiftly than I can. I appreciate that this is because you have fewer fixed attachments and because you accept endings as part of life. Rather, I applaud this and let it inspire me to become more flexible and open to change.

Likewise, I will let you change. I will not hold you to the same way of doing things. I will not let this be a personal threat or a trigger. Shifting is part of who you are.

I promise not to engage with you in the temptations of co-dependency. Our enmeshment will only deplete us both.

I will not block you from exploring alternative forms of spirituality, even if it's not how you were raised or what the community deems acceptable. As long as you are listening to yourself, and not enmeshed with a guru or with group mind, I know you will find your way.

All these I pledge to you, to the best of my human ability. If love is about supporting each other's empowerment, and if everyone has their own path toward that empowerment, then I promise to honor yours, even if it's different than mine.

Signed,

(Your name)

LIVING THE SIGNS
MOON TO MOON

Lunar Rituals for Radiant Embodiment

Working with the Moon means showing up for your self-care, goals, growth, and empowerment in different ways according to the rhythmic, shifting qualities we witness across the 28-day lunar cycle. You might be very familiar with what it means to work with the lunar cycle and have a deep and nourishing practice already. You might have never heard this language before and feel a mix of feelings about whether this is for you. You might be somewhere in between. Moon work is a model that may not work for everyone, and that's okay. If you'd prefer, just think of the rituals that follow as exercises that you can amend to work for your life and your comfort levels.

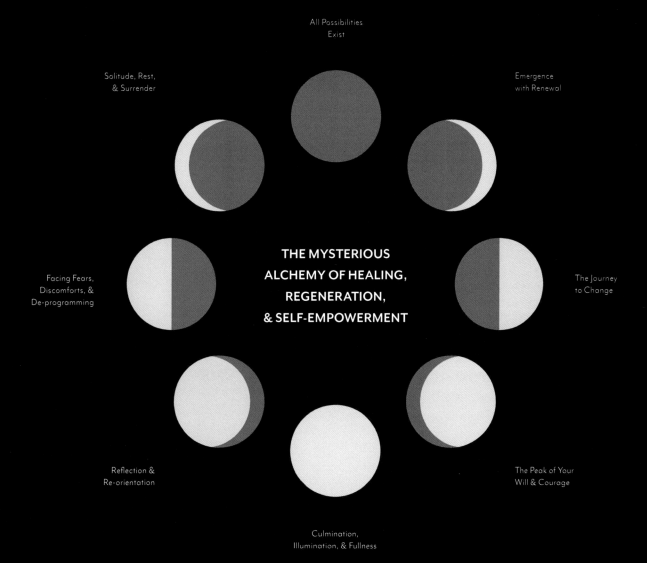

All Possibilities
Exist

Emergence
with Renewal

Solitude, Rest,
& Surrender

THE MYSTERIOUS
ALCHEMY OF HEALING,
REGENERATION,
& SELF-EMPOWERMENT

The Journey
to Change

Facing Fears,
Discomforts, &
De-programming

Reflection &
Re-orientation

The Peak of Your
Will & Courage

Culmination,
Illumination, & Fullness

LUNAR RITUALS FOR LIVING THE SIGNS

Some of the reasons people enjoy working
with the Moon include:

Cultivating the inner voice

Listening to Spirit, Earth, & Cosmos

Touching base with your truth

Setting intentions and nurturing them
for one month at a time

Noticing a healing relationship to time

Trusting in the rightness of rest, play,
and letting go as part of the process
of any cycle

Connecting to the seasons more deeply

Feeling the signs of the zodiac in
real time

Cultivating trust in magic and an
enchanted life

Anchoring through change, which is
the only sure thing

Enjoying the opportunity to work with
candles, the tarot, herbs, oils, crystals
or whatever you might like to bring
into your practice to feel into the time
of the year

My workbook *Moon to Moon: A Journal for Working with the Lunar Cycle* is a deep dive into the language and the practice of lunar rituals and lunar magic. It holds lots of information about the symbolism of the Moon across many traditions, explains the phases of the moon in depth, and has exercises for working with the Moon over four months, one for each of the four elements. Please check that out if you'd like to keep learning. My vision is for it to be companion to this series, as in: *Living the Signs Moon to Moon*. This is a very brief explanation of Moonwork, which deserves more time and space.

The lunar cycle can be divided into any number of phases, but there are two clear points in the cycle upon which we can all agree: the New Moon and the Full Moon. In *Moon to Moon*, I discuss the relevance and importance of other parts of the cycle; herein I just give suggestions for these two parts of the sign season.

The Sun and the Moon have been seen since the ancients as the two luminaries that guide our existence here. What we're doing with Moonwork is noticing and honoring the literal dance between these two. At a symbolic level, the Sun represents our more conscious, goal-driven self, and the Moon represents our more unconscious, hidden, emotionally-driven self. Thus, the New Moon invites us to access both in how we relate to a given sign, skillfully and unskillfully.

A New Moon is when both the Sun and the Moon are together in the sky and thus they are in the same sign, so it's a deep initiation into the energy and teachings of that sign. At the New Moon, the Moon rises with the Sun at dawn, and thus the night sky is Moon-less and full of the most stars in this window.

The New Moon is a period of void, of blank canvas, of starting over and renewal. You can see it as a time for setting intentions and dreams for the lunar cycle to come, and it's most supportive to set goals in the theme of the sign energy of that particular New Moon.

A Full Moon is a time when the Sun and Moon are in opposing signs, so it's a time for balancing parts of self. The Sun is in the same sign at the New Moon but the Moon will be in the polar sign. (See Balancing Pisces with Virgo to learn more about how the zodiac is designed in polarities.) It's also a time mid-lunar cycle when we celebrate and witness all that we've grown, accomplished, and committed to in order to serve our intentions and dreams. We do this as proof of our deep desire to live!

A Full Moon is an excellent time for rituals, parties, and spells relating to wholeness, fulfillment, abundance, manifestation, and culminations. What is ripening is both a sense of the fullness of intentions we set two weeks earlier but also those we set six months before when the Moon was in the New Moon of that sign.

In this way, month to month – Moon to Moon – across the year, you check in with each of the twelve signs, and have conversations with the part of yourself that is each sign, because as you're learning, you are all twelve signs! In this way, you can cultivate more radiant embodiment in a rhythmic journey with organic time. You feel more whole in yourself.

While it is supported and fun to time your attention with the energies of the lunar cycle, know that you can of course engage with and enjoy the following exercises at any time of the year. All you need is the desire to connect with the Pisces within.

A RITUAL WITH PISCES

Swim in Your Own Waters

"Nightswimming deserves a quiet night,
I'm not sure all these people understand."
– R.E.M.

What does that actually look like, swimming in our own waters? To start, think about how it feels to be under water. Submerged, we can't speak. We can't hear very well. Vision is distorted. Movement is slowed, meeting resistance.

When I lived in Hawaii, I finally learned to give into that resistance and simply bob, to float, to just be and see what comes to me, to relax into my fear of the ocean's wildness, to appreciate its altered sense of perception as well as the solitude required to appreciate it.

And so, when I say it's time to swim in our own waters, I mean to truly slow down, to talk less, to say no, to tune people out a little bit. To resist the cultural denigration of naps and

daydreaming. Time that is seemingly "unproductive" can in fact be exactly what we most need to return to our creative source.

I'm not talking about escapism: screens, alcohol, distraction, avoiding all responsibilities. No, I mean conscious, purposeful zoning out. I mean playing and singing to old music you used to love to release the repressed nostalgia. I mean dream-journaling to see what bubbles in your subconscious. I mean staring at your reflection in the bath water until you hear your wise voice speak to you.

Pisces season or not: You are not obligated to anyone to be sociable. Ever.

Sometimes, in these spaces, we recognize the past that we've repressed, or a truth that we need to see. This is often why we avoid alone time in the first place. But this is an absolutely essential part of living through this season.

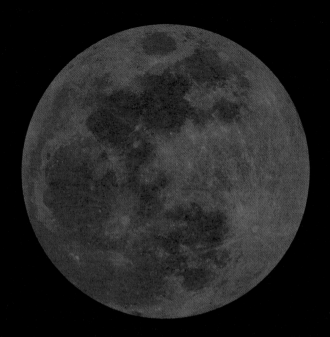

"Nightswimming deserves a quiet night
The photograph on the dashboard, taken
years ago
Turned around backwards so the
windshield shows
Every streetlight reveals the picture
in reverse..."
– R.E.M.

What I've learned is that we must sit gently
with what is uncomfortable: a conversation we
need to have, a fact we need to face, a shame
that shows up in dreams, a wistfulness for a
love lost. We must sit with these with utmost
compassion. (This is the Moon card.) Like
shifting into a yoga pose we think we can't
reach, we must sit with what is uncomfortable
until we gain new perception about it. (This is
the Hanged Man card.)

This new perception may not heal us completely: we can't change the fact of death, or
reverse a loved one's betrayal, or require a
family member to love us unconditionally, but
it can show us the way toward surrendering to
the fact of the past with a more compassionate heart. And in this, we can live with more
presence, we can feel more joy in our process,
and we can crack more open toward
radical self-love.

The end is the beginning, so Pisces teaches us.
And so, it is a time of culminations, of letting
go, of little deaths. And this is not a bad thing.
Why? Because in the letting go, we permission
the start of a new cycle. Aries approaches!
Aries is coming! We must be ready for it.

"The photograph reflects, every streetlight
a reminder
Nightswimming deserves a quiet night,
deserves a quiet night"
- R.E. M.

NEW MOON IN PISCES RITUAL

In honor of the perfectly Piscean R.E.M. song
"Nightswimming", I offer this suggested New Moon in
Pisces ritual, which you can do any day of the year if
you'd rather.

PRE-RITUAL

You'll need:

A few items such as those suggested for the Pisces altar

Candle or multiple candles

This journal and a pen, or colored pens, or watercolors

Labradorite stone to hold in your hand (I find it highly
supportive for intuition and mysticism)

RITUAL

Light your candle(s).

Begin a grounding meditation (contact me if you want a
good one). Establish a strong sense of rootedness. Any
time your mind tries to wander to other thoughts or
people, invite these to leave your space with a hello and
goodbye to well outside your field of vision. Be firm. Fill
yourself with a high and bright light energy from the top of
your head through your body and out your hands, filling
your aura around you. With every breath, let this light loop
get brighter. Invite in any spirit guides, well ancestors, elements, deities, animal guides, or directions that you trust.
Clarify that you seek help only at the highest levels of love
and compassion for all sentient beings. Ask for support in
calling all of yourself back home to you now. Imagine all of
the bits of energy you've left everywhere coming back to
you on a golden web and entering through the top of
your head.

State your intention to work with the Pisces within...
*"I want to go nightswimming. I want to see in the dark.
I want to know what I need to see."*

Now imagine you are in a photography darkroom. In your
hands you hold a piece of white photo paper.

Set your desire to see a picture you are ready to see
("the photograph on the dashboard" in the song).

Allow yourself to see this paper swirling around in the
photo fluids. With every cell of your body, ask to see what
you need to see right now. Perhaps an image from the past,
maybe from the present, possibly in your imagination.
Maybe what you need to see is your dream, your purpose,
your heart's desire.

Let it appear.

Whatever was the first image you saw is perfect.

Now ask yourself: *what do I need to know about this picture? In my heart, what is the photo about?*

How does it make you feel? Is there healing here?

Ask more questions of yourself. Get curious about whatever you saw.

Finish by asking: *What else do I need to know?*

You may not hear language. You may just have feeling sensations in your body. This is normal! Write down everything that came forward for you, including more thoughts, feelings, knowings, sensations, and questions. Draw if you'd rather capture the image with art.

If you work with the tarot, draw a few cards to help you understand what the image wanted to tell you. You can ask:

What is the invitation of this image?
How will this invitation help me?
What else do I need to know?

Journal more or meditate more until you feel completion. At this point, feel into and call up in your body the will and desire to keep nightswimming across the lunar cycle. Say or write down your exact intention.

Thank whatever forces have guided you with this ritual. Feel grateful for your willingness to explore the possibility that this might feel helpful to you.

Feel proud of your bravery to venture into your own "quiet night."

**Ideal for the Full Moon in Virgo
in Pisces Season**

A RITUAL WITH PISCES

The Beauty is in the Details

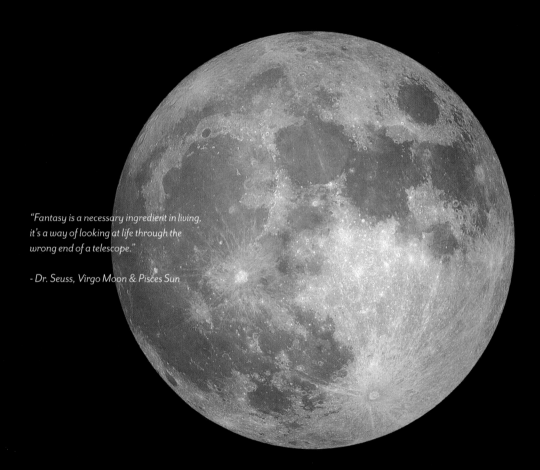

*"Fantasy is a necessary ingredient in living,
it's a way of looking at life through the
wrong end of a telescope."*

- Dr. Seuss, Virgo Moon & Pisces Sun

Now is the time when you witness, honor, and celebrate all that you've achieved and grown since the New Moon in Virgo in late August and early September. (Or, just do this any time of year in order to connect with Virgo-Pisces).

The Full Moon in Virgo is a Magnifying Glass.

To be in balance with Pisces-Virgo energy, let us dilate the infinite in the little things.

Let us make our daily routine more spiritually charged.

Let us recognize the strange beauty of the everyday through the magnification of the details.

Let us lose track of time by contemplating the patterns in a lover's pupil.

The tendency with opposing signs in our psyche is to be in one energy and not the other, to compartmentalize. Either be all vastness or all efficiency, at any given time. Let us rather seek the balance at the center.

"Grandeur progresses in the world in proportion to the deepening of intimacy."

This is one of my favorite lines from a favorite book: *The Poetics of Space* by Gaston Bachelard. I encourage you to say it to yourself as many times as you need to in order for its essence to sink in.

Virgo-Pisces balance is about playing with spatial dimension in our lives and psyches. To magnify the grandeur of the intimacies of our daily life is to invite in wonder, gratitude, and Spirit.

For this ritual, find a quiet space where you enjoy being alone and meditating, perhaps your altar.

Bring this journal and pen.

Light a candle.

Give yourself a grounding meditation and call in your highest energy of self-love and self-trust.

What is coming up for me right now? Emotionally, spiritually, physically, mentally?

What have I been able to manifest with intention lately?

Consider all that you've been learning about Pisces, and hold Pisces in balance with what you know about the Virgo archetype. See pages 50-53 for guidance.

Name at least three qualities of Pisces energy that you are consciously working with or want to call in right now. For each of these, ask how Virgo energy can serve you and help you at this time with what you are dreaming into being? Be practical. Be specific with the details.

If you enjoy the tarot, you can weave your cards into this ritual by pulling one card for each Pisces trait you want to magnify and then pull 3 cards for suggested actions that bring Virgo pragmatism to this process.

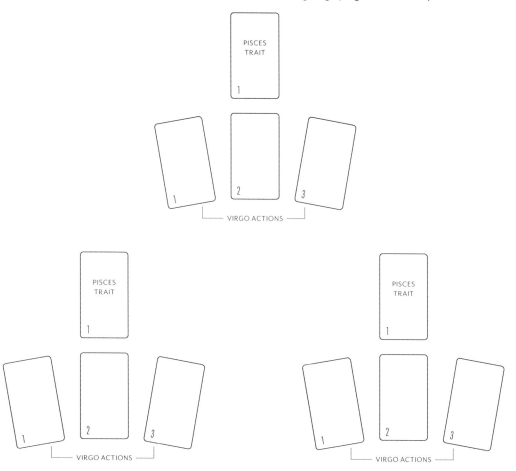

This activity is a riff on a suggested tarot spread by Sarah Faith Gottesdiener in the July-December 2018 edition of Many Moons.

Note your insights and let the spread continue to talk to you over the coming days and weeks.

Full Moons are a great time to celebrate our successes, big and small. What have you nurtured into being since September when there was a Virgo New Moon? What have you put out there? What have you cultivated? How have you shifted? How can you re-align and re-center to your autumn goals?

Notice what shows up in this exercise, and make time to celebrate.

Celebrate Virgo-Pisces style: By taking a magnifying glass to your life and seeing the details anew.

Delight in the minutiae of your daily self-care.

Dilate the mysticism of your daily routine.

Enlarge the hidden grandeur of your rituals through contemplation.

Thank whatever forces are guiding you right now. Promise to tune into them more often.

Happy Full Moon!

A RITUAL WITH PISCES

Bless the Feet that Got You Here

Some six months after the New Moon in Pisces, you enjoy the flowering of your intention across the spring and summer cycles reflected back to you in the Pisces Full Moon during Virgo season. What a joy! What a celebration! What a harvest of dreams!

When the Sun is in Virgo, life is busy. It's late August and the first half of September, and you are getting it all done. Back to school. Back to work. Back on task. You are in full force.

The Moon waxes from its promising start, and you wake up every day in service to what you devote yourself to bringing in the world, trying to do things better, cleaner, more efficiently.

So, when the Moon bloats to its full ripeness across 3 nights in the opposing sign of Pisces, it is a time to pause in wonder. The Moon shimmers and glows, and magnetizes your heart to the sky. It is my favorite Moon of the year! She is never so glorious to me as she is in Pisces.

Do you remember what your heart seeded back at the New Moon in Pisces in late Feb or early March? What was ending and moving to the number 13 (Mysteries - Death)? What was beginning and inviting in the energy of number 1 (Magician - Aries)?

Whatever were the dreams you determined to stop deferring, now is the time to witness, honor, and celebrate all that you've done to will and (hu-)manifest them into reality.

The following ritual is about connecting the earth (Virgo) to your feet and intuition (Pisces). The exercise is inspired by the connection between Pisces and its planetary ruler Neptune. In medical astrology, Neptune corresponds to the pineal gland, and Pisces corresponds to the feet. The pineal gland is the source of your intuition in the brain space. The receptors across the bottom of the feet (along with the palms of the hands) are sites for receiving intuitive information that you process at the pineal gland. It's important to be barefoot regularly in order to receive the energy of the earth. For this ritual, you will want to be barefoot.

Your feet do so much! They are flexible and amazing parts of the body, but – like all of us – our feet can carry unprocessed trauma.

You may be surprised by what comes up with this ritual. My mother's mother lived with Multiple Sclerosis. I loved my grandmother so much. It was hard to watch her get increasingly immobile. I felt guilty when she couldn't go with us places. I accepted and surrendered to the fact that she couldn't see me do all the things I did and be active with me. She never complained, so why would I?

And so, in the process of my inner work, it shouldn't have taken me by surprise (but it did) to discover I carried mixed feelings about my legs and feet. I've worked on healing a dis-ease with my lower limbs, leaning into trusting I can let them take me places, and healing the inherited trauma of a body that is stuck in one place. Yes, we carry the struggles of our lineage in our bodies. I am now a marathon runner and I actively live my dreams in my reality. So, yes – this is worth it! And yes, my grandmother is cheering me on!

FOR THIS RITUAL, YOU WILL

"There can be a progression to the dream; there can be steps to it. When you dissect any successful person's story, it's really rare that it was all or nothing. It's steps, and I just try to remind myself of that in terms of the things that I want; it's like, everything is a step, leading you to where you need to go."

– Ava DuVernay, Virgo Sun & Pisces Moon Pisces Moon

WANT TO GATHER:

A picnic blanket

Massage oil or lotion with a self-supporting essence like rose (but any will do if you don't have time!)

This journal and pen

Firelight of some kind

This ritual ideally takes place outdoors so look to the weather and pick a night within the Full Moon window when this will make the most sense. If the outdoor elements are not cooperating, then pick a room or space where you can still see the Moon.

This is a gorgeous ritual to do with a loving, supportive, safe, empathic partner, if you desire it.

RITUAL

Lay out your blanket where you can sit under the Moon. Set up a fire in an outdoor pit or with candles.

Meditate enough to securely ground and root into the earth, and call back your energy from the day.

Invite in the support of the most loving guides, ancestors, and deities that you trust. Whatever works for you here. Invite in the voice of your intuition, your higher self.

Now, call up the energy of your deepest dream(s), feel it infuse your heart first and then grow out to every cell of your body. Start with whatever comes first and then listen to what wants to bubble up. Let this be intuitive and not analytical. There is no right or wrong. Feel full and infused with your heart's longings and your spirit's dreams before the next step.

Now turn your attention to your feet.

Notice if you have mixed feelings about them, which can happen if you have or have had any injury there. If you are unhappy with where your life has taken you, even at an unconscious level, it would be normal to "blame" your feet in some way. This can even happen if your feet are healthy, if there's a story in your family about unhealthy limbs, as in mine.

If you know you need healing here, fill yourself and your feet with the highest levels of self-compassion you can muster. This will be the healing of this ritual then, feeling gratitude for your own self-compassion. Let the Moon help you.

If you are ready to bless and give thanks for your feet, then fill yourself with the highest levels of love and gratitude for them. Thank the universe for all that you've moved through since late winter, trusting that even the hard stuff brought some kind of learning and wisdom that will serve your future self and your dreams. Let the Moon inspire you.

There is a connection between how you feel about your feet, and your willingness to receive from them. The more you can open your relationship with them, the more you can intuit and see your dreams.

At this point, you are invited to massage your feet as long as feels right. Let the Moon's soft and loving light guide your hands. If you are not able to massage your feet, and/or if you are doing this with someone else, let them massage your feet for you.

Anointing the feet with oil, blessing them, and massaging them – these are ancient acts of respect and love. Be in reverence to this ritual. This is really big magic.

If you have a partner that you trust completely and with whom you feel fully yourself, I invite you to kiss, touch, and make love under the Full Moon afterwards. If not, then let the Moon love on you. Be in wonder at how magical and beautiful you are, how incredible it is to be alive, how poignant it is to be human.

Blessed be! Thank you, Moon! We love you!

EPILOGUE

We hope you enjoyed working with this book.

We hope you learned some ways to support yourself with the language of astrology, the tarot, energy healing, and lunar cycles.

We hope you had experiences of clearly hearing your inner voice.

We hope you trust more completely that change is not only possible, it is natural and good.

We hope you had profound "aha" moments where you realized that the behaviors and patterns about your life that have long frustrated you were always just past-tense leftovers from the survival needs of your younger self, and that you can now rewire to the present moment by gaining new tools and changing your circumstances.

We hope you see that you are magic, you are cosmos, and you are not alone.

What next?

Living the Signs is meant to anchor you throughout the year as the Sun moves around the zodiac. If you loved working with this book, we invite you to check out the others in this series and you can return to them year after year.

We also have a workbook called *Moon to Moon*. Whereas the *Living the Signs* books develop deep self-understanding with the wisdom of each sign and its ruling planet, *Moon to Moon* focuses more on the practical application of self-healing and empowerment in lunar time. Together they build and weave the What with the How of cultivating empowering change, de-programming, and growing abundant radiance. We encourage you to check that out if the themes from this workbook resonate with you.

If you would like to go deeper into work with sign wisdom, please keep an eye out for any workshops, newsletters, podcast episodes, or classes Britten offers throughout the year to guide folks with embodying this wisdom more deeply. You might also consider working with Britten one-on-one for astrological life coaching and/or mystical business mentorship.

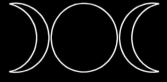

JOURNALING PAGES

APPENDIX
WITH
RESOURCES

THE TWELVE HOUSES

Here we have an amalgamation of various standard diagrams for the 12 Houses.

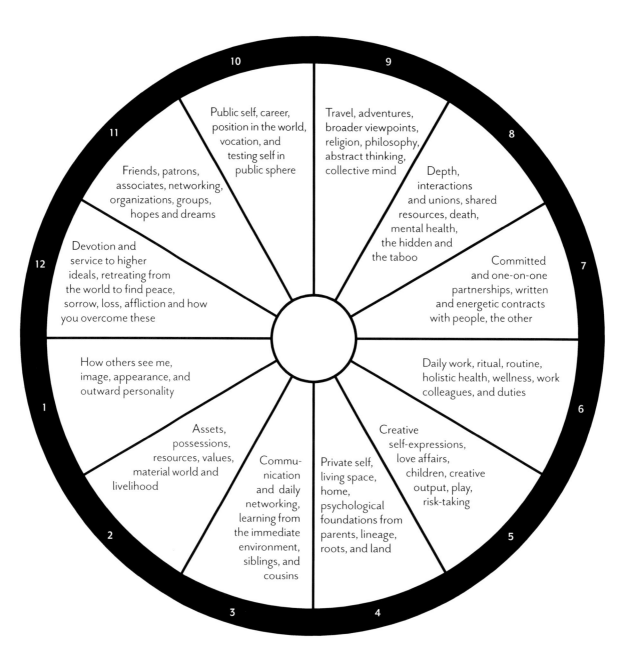

10 — Public self, career, position in the world, vocation, and testing self in public sphere

9 — Travel, adventures, broader viewpoints, religion, philosophy, abstract thinking, collective mind

11 — Friends, patrons, associates, networking, organizations, groups, hopes and dreams

8 — Depth, interactions and unions, shared resources, death, mental health, the hidden and the taboo

12 — Devotion and service to higher ideals, retreating from the world to find peace, sorrow, loss, affliction and how you overcome these

7 — Committed and one-on-one partnerships, written and energetic contracts with people, the other

1 — How others see me, image, appearance, and outward personality

6 — Daily work, ritual, routine, holistic health, wellness, work colleagues, and duties

2 — Assets, possessions, resources, values, material world and livelihood

5 — Creative self-expressions, love affairs, children, creative output, play, risk-taking

3 — Communication and daily networking, learning from the immediate environment, siblings, and cousins

4 — Private self, living space, home, psychological foundations from parents, lineage, roots, and land

THE HOUSES AS SPACES FOR SELF-HEALING

This is an original diagram of my own making. It depicts how I consider each house as a personal space where we can realign and heal from unskillful or harmful patterning. Please do not copy or publish this diagram without citing my name. Copyright © 2020 Britten LaRue

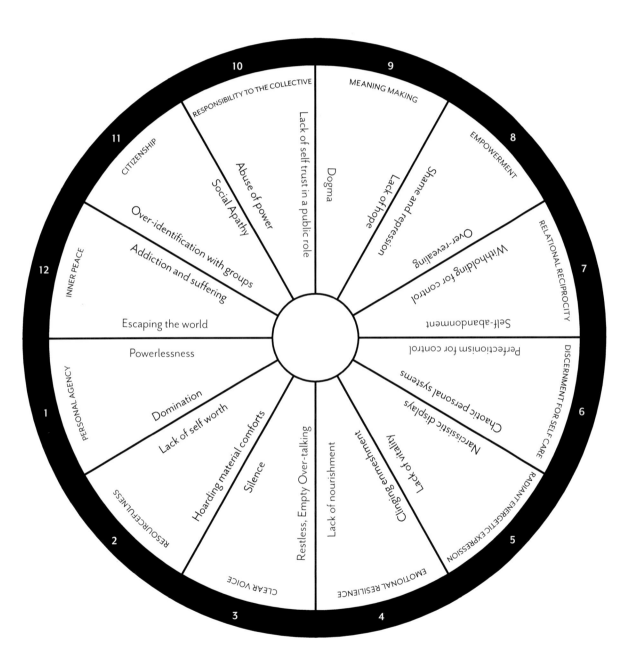

SIGN PHRASES & ADJECTIVES

My approach to seeing the application of signs as "skillful" and "unskillful" comes from Demetra George and Douglas Bloch's wonderful book Astrology for Yourself. *The keyphrases here are nearly direct quotes from their text. I encourage anyone interested in going deeper into astrology to purchase their workbook.*

♈ ARIES

KEYPHRASE: My need to be independent and develop personal initiative.

SKILLFUL ADJECTIVES: Initiating, Pioneering, Courageous, Daring, Active, Inspiring, Direct, Energetic, Exuberant

UNSKILLFUL ADJECTIVES: Reckless, Uncooperative, Coarse, Combative, Domineering

♉ TAURUS

KEYPHRASE: My need to be resourceful, productive, and stable.

SKILLFUL ADJECTIVES : Practical, Sensual, Determined, Loyal, Artistic, Prudent, Persevering, Patient, Deliberate, Consistent

UNSKILLFUL ADJECTIVES
Possessive, Overcautious, Bull-headed, Fixed, Sluggish

♊ GEMINI

KEYPHRASE: My need to communicate with and learn from others.

SKILLFUL ADJECTIVES: Mental, Communicative, Talkative, Sociable, Witty, Inquisitive, Literary, Logical, Studious, Curious

UNSKILLFUL ADJECTIVES: Spacey, Superficial, Fickle, Nosy, Gossipy

♋ CANCER

KEYPHRASE: My need to give and receive emotional warmth and security.

SKILLFUL ADJECTIVES: Receptive, Feeling, Protective, Tenacious, Providing, Gentle, Psychic, Vulnerable, Sympathetic, Patriotic

UNSKILLFUL ADJECTIVES: Defensive, Hypersensitive, Clinging, Overprotective, Clannish

♌ LEO

KEYPHRASE: My need to creatively express myself and be appreciated by others.

SKILLFUL ADJECTIVES: Self-confident, Dynamic, Proud, Big-hearted, Generous, Regal, Courageous, Authoritative, Radiant, Romantic

UNSKILLFUL ADJECTIVES: Vain, Overbearing, Dictatorial, Egocentric, Melodramatic

♍ VIRGO

KEYPHRASE: My need to analyze, discriminate, and function efficiently.

SKILLFUL ADJECTIVES: Practical, Efficient, Disciplined, Detailed, Precise, Technical, Skillful, Helpful, Analytical, Problem-solving

UNSKILLFUL ADJECTIVES: Picky, Fault-finding, Perfectionistic, Neurotic, Self-denying

LIBRA

KEYPHRASE: My need to cooperate with others and to create beauty, balance, and harmony.

SKILLFUL ADJECTIVES: Relating, Social, Charming, Tactful, Diplomatic, Cooperative, Artistic, Tasteful, Impartial, Mediating

UNSKILLFUL ADJECTIVES: Dependent, Indecisive, Passive, Superficial, Overly delicate

 SCORPIO

KEYPHRASE: My need for deep involvements and intense transformation.

SKILLFUL ADJECTIVES: Complex, Probing, Piercing, Magnetic, Mysterious, Deep, Healing, Erotic, Sharp, Psychological

UNSKILLFUL ADJECTIVES: Jealous, Obsessive Destructive, Secretive, Suspicious

 SAGITTARIUS

KEYPHRASE: My need to explore and expand the horizons of my mind and world.

SKILLFUL ADJECTIVES: Wise, Philosophical, Exploring, Freedom-loving, Athletic, Optimistic, Benevolent, Expansive, Generous, Loves animals

UNSKILLFUL ADJECTIVES: Condescending, Dogmatic, Zealous, Exaggerating, Insensitive

 CAPRICORN

KEYPHRASE: My need for structure, organization, and social accomplishment.

SKILLFUL ADJECTIVES: Organized, Pragmatic, Cautious, Dutiful, Industrious, Striving, Ambitious Methodical, Reserved, Structured

UNSKILLFUL ADJECTIVES: Controlling, Rigid, Unimaginative, Opportunistic, Distrustful

 AQUARIUS

KEYPHRASE: My need to be innovative, original, and to create social change.

SKILLFUL ADJECTIVES: Reforming, Humanitarian, Gregarious, Independent, Unusual, Innovative, Brilliant, Scientific, Progressive, Tolerant

UNSKILLFUL ADJECTIVES: Opinionated, Impractical, Negligent, Inconsistent, Aloof

PISCES

KEYPHRASE: My need to commit myself to a dream or ideal and work toward its realization.

SKILLFUL ADJECTIVES: Poetic, Romantic, Visionary, Ethereal, Sensitive, Empathic, Otherworldly, Compassionate, Dreamy, Humble

UNSKILLFUL ADJECTIVES: Confused, Ungrounded, Self-destructive, Melancholic, Suffering

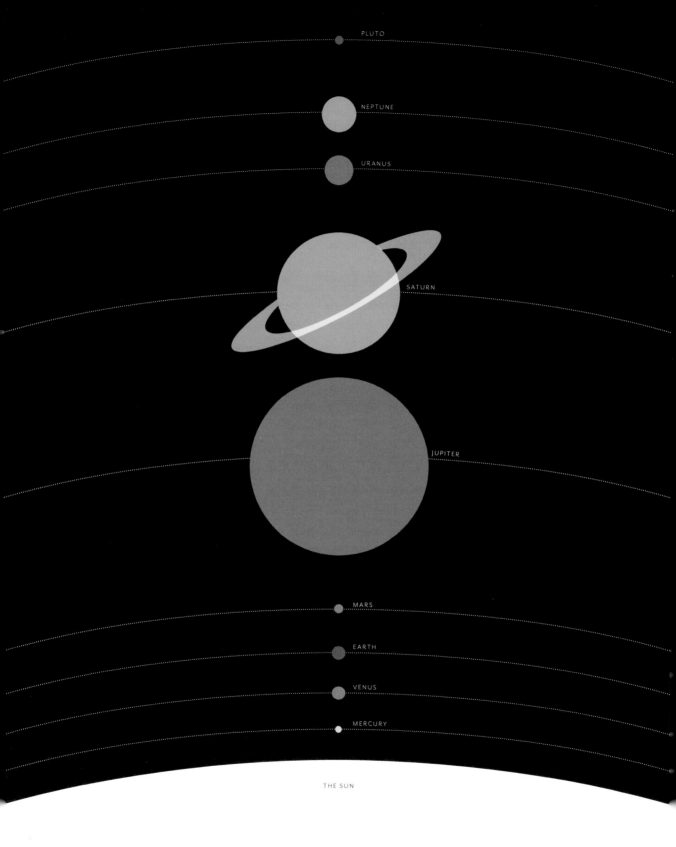

PLUTO

NEPTUNE

URANUS

SATURN

JUPITER

MARS

EARTH

VENUS

MERCURY

THE SUN

LIVING THE SIGNS

PLANETS AND SYMBOLS

☉ SUN: My basic identity, my will, my creative purpose, my vitality, and my authority in the world

☽ MOON: My emotional body, my intuition, and my daily habits

☿ MERCURY: My intellect and my capacity to think, communicate, rationalize, and learn

♀ VENUS: How I love, and my capacity to attract people and things that I love and value

♂ MARS: My assertiveness, my energy, and my capacity to act and assert myself based on personal desire

♃ JUPITER: My enthusiasm, my optimism, and my capacity for meaning, truth, and ethical values

♄ SATURN: The shape of my life's lessons and my capacity to create order, form, and discipline in my life

♅ URANUS: My eccentricity, my uniqueness, my capacity to liberate myself from past limitations

♆ NEPTUNE: My dreams and illusions, and my capacity for transcendence and connection to a greater whole

♇ PLUTO: My capacity to transform and renew myself through ego surrender

⚷ CHIRON: My capacity to integrate mind and body, and to transform past wounds into healing

AC RISING SIGN: How I express my personality, how others see me, and the vehicle for my purpose

☊ NORTH NODE: The direction of my soul's growth, where I hunger to evolve, and what might feel challenging

☋ SOUTH NODE: My innate talents, resources, and abilities that are comfortable and familiar to me

*Much of the language on this spread was
inspired by the workbook *Astrology for Yourself*
by Demetra George and Douglas Bloch.

TIPS FOR STARTING A TAROT PRACTICE

BUYING A DECK

First, you have to consider what matters most to you.

If you want to understand the visual history of the tarot, in terms of canonical images that most people understand as common language, and that most modern decks reference and interrogate in some way, then I would start with the Centennial version of the Smith-Rider-Waite deck.

If you want a deck that is easy to intuit based on the images, then I recommend The Wild Unknown by Kim Krans, because it's the one that taught me first, and I found it came quickly. The figures in every card are non-human, which was helpful as a ground base for my practice.

If you want a deck that is created by a living, independent artist, and seek resources about makers, check out @indiedeckreview on IG. littleredtarot.com also has loads of decks to study to get an idea of the visual range that's out there. Look for decks that resonate with you, for art that pulls at your heart, for a sense of "that's my deck."

If you are looking for a deck that actively does not center white, cis, hetero, young, skinny folks, then there are lots of decks out there. It's a matter of looking around. asaliearthwork.com has a list of decks for QTPOC. See also browngirltarot.com for a growing database of decks that were created by and/or include people of color. I personally recommend the decks Next World, Sasuraibito, and Modern Witch for your consideration.

Tarot thought-leader Lindsay Mack once said that one should approach purchasing a tarot deck with the anticipation and reverence of beginning a long and deep friendship. So, ultimately, just listen to your inner voice that knows which deck you want.

PULLING CARDS

Shuffle the cards in a manner that feels natural. I hold the whole deck in my right hand and lift cards up and drop down with my left. Whatever you do is perfect. This part of the process is a practice in focus, will, and intention while also staying soft and open.

Feel into the question you want to ask and let it infuse your whole body through your hands to the cards. I like to start or end my question with "for my highest and best, at the highest levels of love and compassion for all sentient beings."

And then when I feel a sense of completion (this is just intuitive and organic like knowing you're done eating), I cut the deck into three piles and say "I am open and I'm listening."

This is where people differ depending on their intuitive inclinations. I used to then get a feeling sense in my body which pile to draw from and I'd take the top card. This is perfect and normal. Now I hear a clear number, meaning which number from the top, and I get a knowing about which pile, and I follow that. About 6 months into practicing with the deck I noticed I heard numbers, and this was a natural evolution of building trust in my intuition.

My advice is to lovingly allow your intuition to teach you this process over time and with practice. The most important thing is not to second guess yourself. It's the first feeling you have. That's how intuition works! It's your analytical brain that jumps in to get you doubting yourself. You have to train yourself to trust the first feeling.

This whole process here speaks to how helpful the tarot is in building self-trust.

GUIDANCE FOR INTERPRETATION

You will likely have a feeling sense right away about what the card is trying to tell you, vis-à-vis your question. If not, then turn to the guidebook you're using to help you. Take notes. Over time, you will have cards that repeat and you will build a relationship with each card. Only across time will you know all 78 of them. Only with organic practice by building relationship to each one as they apply to your lived experience and lived truth. Eventually, some of the cards may mean something to you very different from accepted "meanings," and this is totally okay.

It is my strong recommendation that, if you are new to the tarot, you begin by pulling one card a day and learning slowly as you practice, rather than trying to understand all of them at the beginning. This simple way can help you get going, trusting that the process will take the time it needs. Most modern decks have a decent guidebook that comes along with the deck. Combine the most general, most helpful, most medicinal possibility given by the guidebook and then combine that meaning with your own gut feeling looking at the card.

Throughout this book, I prompt with questions, and then ask you to consider what feels true for you. As you contemplate and journal, you will come to an idea of what a card "means" for you in that moment. Know that what the card wanted to tell you will continue to evolve over time as you witness its energies play out in your life.

There are book and podcast recommendations on the Resources page for further learning. Online, I used the meanings given at *biddytarot.com* when I was first starting, because her language seemed sensible and helpful. Discernment is the key when it comes to selecting sources. Avoid writers that promote fear and crazy predictions. As a general rule, I don't entertain explanations of cards that suggest they are about other people. All cards that you pull are about you.

Here is a list of tarot readers and/or teachers on Instagram who I follow and admire:

@meridiantarot	@angelamarymagick
@staywoketarot	@oracleofla
@aceoftarot	@wildsoulhealing
@soundartmagic	@daughter.of.wands
@goldynfinch	@ddamascenaa
@hijaquecura	@gottesss
@erynj_	@vardotarot
@riseupgoodwitch	@sincerely_the_tarot
@brooklyntarot	@thehoodwitch
@politicsoftarot	@marcellakroll
@mallorydowd	@lalobalocashares
@insearchoftarot	@thetarotlady

This list is not meant to be exhaustive or definitive.

Don't forget to have fun!

RESOURCES

INTUITION, MOON GUIDANCE, ASTROLOGY, AND TAROT

I could list so many more, but these are my primary teachers. I have paid them for their one-on-one or course-based guidance. I completed training with the first two listed. Everybody listed here is a critical thinker invested in shaping their fields in innovative ways. Everybody listed here is also deeply invested in relearning how to work in partnership with nature as well as deprogramming from a lot of the toxic conditioning of modern life.

Deborah Kremins: intuitionmed.com (medical intuitive, teacher)

Adam Sommer: holestoheavens.com (astrology, teacher, podcast wizard)

Achintya Devi: goddessrising.org (leader of women's groups in shamanistic and goddess-based wisdom)

Sarah Faith Gottesdiener: visualmagic.info (moon teacher and very smart writer and thinker)

Lindsay Mack: lindsaymack.com (creator of Soul Tarot and teacher by podcast and courses)

Amanda Yates Garcia: oracleoflosangeles.com (writer, healer, reader, podcast maven on tarot and magical practices)

Lara Veleda Vesta: laravesta.co (writer, teacher of the runes, and guide to helping us heal the witch wound)

Natasha Levinger: highestlighthealing.com (intuitive energy reader and healer, inner child healing expert)

Luis Mojica: holisticlifenavigation.com (somatic therapist, life coach, whole food nutritional counselor)

BOOKS

Caroline W. Casey, *Visionary Activist Astrology* (audiobook on Audible, my favorite text on the subject)

Robert Cole and Paul Williams, *The Book of Houses: An Astrological Guide to the Harvest Cycle in Human Life*

Swami Kriyananda, *Your Sun Sign as a Spiritual Guide* (short but deep)

Demetra George, *Astrology and the Authentic Self* (very wise; not for beginners)

Demetra George and Douglas Bloch, *Astrology for Yourself* (workbook for beginners)

Alejandro Jodorowsky, *The Way of the Tarot: The Spiritual Teacher in the Cards*

Mary K. Greer, *Tarot for Your Self*

Chani Nicholas, *You Were Born for This: Astrology for Radical Self-Acceptance* (newly published text for beginners by a modern master)

Rachel Pollack, *Tarot Wisdom: Spiritual Teachings and Deeper Meanings*

Howard Sasportas, *The Twelve Houses: Exploring the Houses of the Horoscope* (great book to get deeper into the houses and planets)

Richard Tarnas, *Cosmos and Psyche: Intimations of a New World View* (serious and scholarly)

adrienne maree brown, *Pleasure Activism: The Politics of Feeling Good*

... and, of course, the other books in this *Living the Signs* workbook series

PODCASTS

Holes to Heavens

Cosmic Cousins

Embodied Astrology

Anne Ortelee's Weekly Weather

Tarot for the Wild Soul

Between the Worlds

Living Open

The Astrology Podcast

Moon to Moon

Holistic Life Navigation

How to Survive the End of the World

Magic Monday

LIVING THE SIGNS

About the Collaboration

Living the Signs: Astrology for Radiant Embodiment is a series of twelve workbooks created by astrologer Britten LaRue and designer Angela George. Each book is an invitation to dive deep into the teachings of a single sign with journaling prompts, suggested exercises, tarot spreads, and lunar rituals designed to inspire the reader to interact with and practice more engaged embodiment with the world of wisdom that is each sign. What is especially notable about the series is how each book engages the reader on so many levels: aesthetically, mentally, emotionally, and even spiritually.

The project began when astro-curious Angela sought out Britten's guidance for personal readings and courses. Angela quickly fell in love with Britten's teaching style and would often journal and expand upon Britten's words with her own artwork and graphic visual interpretations of the material.

Britten was so inspired by the way her words looked through Angela's artful interpretations that she suggested they meet for tea. The two immediately bonded over their shared love for journaling as an anchor for self-care and as a canvas for the imagination. That very day, they dreamed up multiple collaborative projects, the first of which became the first edition of *Living the Signs: Pisces*.

The idea blossomed from Britten's unique approach to teaching sign wisdom as invitations to connect with all parts of who we are. She developed this way of thinking about signs while deeply engaged in self-healing work with her own chart, her tarot decks, a deeply connected lunar ritual practice, and her many, many journals for logging every dream, thought, feeling, "aha" moment, fear, and intuitive download. With her long background in teaching, Britten began to visualize how she might engage others to experiment with working with the signs from her perspective, and she found in Angela a muse to manifest words into form.

Britten and Angela are a collaboration designed by the stars, you might say. Britten is Aries Rising and Angela is Libra Rising, and these are polar signs. Polar signs are seemingly opposite, but they are really like two sides of the same coin. Thus, they support each other to be more balanced and evolved. On the spectrum between total self-sufficiency and total dependency, Angela and Britten constantly engage each other to bring both bravado and beauty to their co-creations, to try new things and also be wise about their choices, to push to the deadlines and not compromise on good design, to want what they each want while also bowing to one another in deep respect.

More than this, Britten's Pisces Sun, Mercury, & Venus are opposite Angela's Virgo Moon, Mercury, & Venus, again activating a key polarity. Angela's close attention to detail balances Britten's intuitive expansiveness. Angela is able to attune so closely to Britten's sensibility that she can make visible what is largely conceptual, felt, or imagined.

And finally, Britten and Angela have important connections between each other's Saturn placements. Saturn is the principle that teaches us discipline and constriction. Why? In order to manifest on the physical plane. Until we give something form, it doesn't exist in a way that can be useful to anyone. Saturn speaks to long-term commitments and building things that withstand the tests of time and resistance. Angela's Saturn in Libra inspires Britten's Jupiter in Gemini to make words that really matter. Britten's Saturn in Leo inspires Angela's Neptune in Sagittarius to design the cosmic dream. Despite the pressures of 2020, these are two collaborators who show up with sincere devotion and loving commitment to what they want to see made in the world.

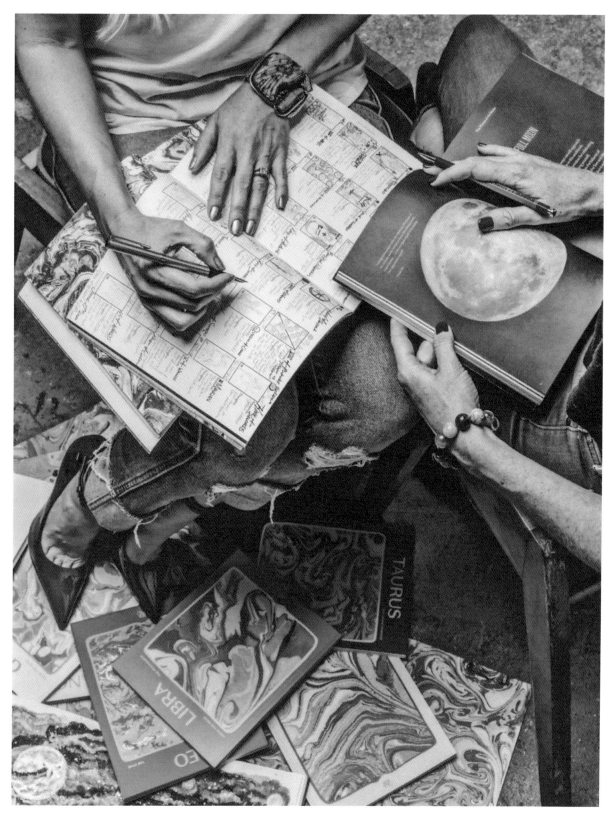

LIVING THE SIGNS

ABOUT IN CASE OF EMERGENCE

At In Case of Emergence, we create tools and opportunities for calling in and listening to what we call The Emergent Self. The emergent self is always in the process of unfolding, of discovering, of remembering who we are. The emergent self trusts that this process is natural and possesses its own wisdom, timing, and beauty... like the tides, like the cycles of the seasons.

We prefer "emergent self" over the term "aspirational self" because when you privilege the aspirational self you focus on a future version of who you are that by implication isn't here now. You are thus always hustling to be something external to you, and in the present, feel a lack. Emergence, by contrast, happens always in the present moment. It's about listening and "becoming approachable," as Turner says, to the you that is mysterious and exciting because not fully revealed. This is much more empowering as a model.

Astrology is one tool among many with which In Case of Emergence engages to support you in becoming approachable to the you that is emerging.

TITLES

Living the Signs: Aries, The Warrior

Living the Signs: Taurus, The Sensuous One

Living the Signs: Gemini, The Storyteller

Living the Signs: Cancer, The Psychic

Living the Signs: Leo, The Star

Living the Signs: Virgo,The Devoted One

Living the Signs: Libra, The Peacemaker

Living the Signs: Scorpio, The Alchemist

Living the Signs: Sagittarius, The Seeker

Living the Signs: Capricorn, The Enduring One

Living the Signs: Aquarius, The Visionary

Living the Signs: Pisces, The Dreamer

Moon to Moon: A Journal for Working with the Lunar Cycle

Seeding the Year, 2020

Seeding the Year, 2021

Seeding the Year, 2022

In Case of Emergence titles can be purchased at our website or in boutique shops across the country. If you are a retailer interested in wholesale orders, please connect with us!

"Emergence never happens all at once. It is a slow stepping into the expanded capacity of your next self. You may need practice at releasing in those places you've grown accustomed to bracing which, like a tight swaddle, was comforting in its limits. But when the time to remain hidden comes to its natural end, you must begin to inhabit your new dimensionality, breathe into the fullness of your gaining altitude and consider that what presents itself as fear may actually be exhilaration. As your future approaches you, worry less how it may receive you and say a prayer instead for your becoming approachable."

– Toko-pa Turner, Belonging: Remembering Ourselves Home

ABOUT BRITTEN LARUE

Britten LaRue is a Dallas native with a long history of academic and museum work in art history, including over a decade of university teaching experience. She used to research, write, and speak about aspects of visual culture that reveal the gender and sexual politics inherent in social history. Understanding power dynamics has always been the underlying focus of whatever she does.

A few years ago, Britten walked away from academia in a period of massive change when the moon started talking to her and she woke up to her natural abilities as a mystic. Seduced and exhilarated by her her own bravery, she started becoming the dream of her younger self. And she magnetizes those who crave the same experience of emergence. Now she is a transformational life guide and magical business coach. She supports her community primarily with technologies of intuitive listening, which include wisdom she receives from astrology and the tarot.

Born with the life card The Hierophant, Britten is the creator of Emergence Astrology, which leans on this ancient symbolic language to help us become approachable to the self and the wild path that is emerging in the dark for us. Welding the analytical with the mystical, the mundane with the magical, the cosmos with the heart, Emergence

Astrology is a practice of deep listening. The goal of Emergence Astrology is to become more trusting of the wild path that wants to be illuminated. As Britten likes to say: "To people hungry for answers, Emergence Astrology will never give them to you."

Britten is Aries Rising with a Pisces Sun and Capricorn Moon. What that means is that she inspires with her courage, determination, and independence. This approach to life helps her serve her larger purpose, which is to offer her empathic and intuitive gifts to help others transcend their past and follow their dreams. She nurtures this purpose with an underlying need to be achieving, disciplined, and focused.

Britten hosts a podcast called *Moon to Moon* (found on iTunes or Spotify), where she shares her thoughts about astrology, the tarot, intuition, energy healing, and lunar cycles with a wider audience. You can also find her at *brittenlarue.com* and follow her on Instagram at @brittenlarue.

ABOUT ANGELA GEORGE

Angela is a creative director and branding maven living in Dallas, Texas. She has walked numerous companies through the branding exercise, both young enterprises and established brands looking for a fresh identity.

At the core of her practice is always strategic, conceptual, design work. Her innovative outlook allows clients to articulate their unique qualities in ways that forge profound and lasting connections, which she then translates through the language of design.

Angela founded her design company By George Partners in 2011 to focus her energy on the clientele she is most passionate about— lifestyle brands with an emphasis on food, fashion, and hospitality industries.

In 2019 she leapt into a new adventure with her husband Matt (another astrological match woven by the stars if there ever was one). Together they opened Lagoon studio in the Dallas Design District. The 4,000 sq. ft. warehouse studio is a multifaceted space that serves as a blank canvas for creatives to make and create for their highest and best.

Angela is a Leo Sun, Virgo Moon, and Libra Rising, meaning this shining Leo star is motivated by her Libran desire to create harmonious beauty in everything she touches. With her Virgo Moon there is a longing to be of service to these details, and it comes naturally to her to quickly discern, analyze and understand what clients need and how she can use her gifts to celebrate and create for them.

Angela is a devout student of these workbooks as much as she is the designer. She has just as much fun devouring the content and exploring in the rituals, as she does crafting the spreads and deciphering the information to present for each new book.

With so much swirling around this vivacious business owner, it's practices like these of turning to the stars, aligning with the tarot, and a daily yoga routine that help to keep her mind focused and heart centered. You can follow along with her company's adventures on Instagram @bygeorgepartners, or check in with what's happening at the studio @inlagoon.